The Natural Touch:

Reaching Others for Christ

Kim Swithinbank

Marshall Pickering

Marshall Morgan and Scott
Marshall Pickering
3 Beggarwood Lane, Basingstoke, Hants RG23 7LP, UK

Copyright © 1988 Kim Swithinbank
First published in 1988 by Marshall Morgan and Scott Publications Ltd
Part of the Marshall Pickering Holdings Group
A subsidiary of the Zondervan Corporation

ISBN 0-551-01616-7

Text Set in Plantin by Brian Robinson, Buckingham
Printed in Great Britain by Anchor Brendon Ltd., Colchester, Essex

Contents

Acknowledgements

Many people have influenced my thinking about the subject of reaching others for Christ. Perhaps especially in the context of this book that influence has been particularly significant in a group we run at All Souls called 'Open to Question'. Both the members of the group and its leaders have contributed a great deal to my understanding of the importance of taking seriously the questions that many raise about Christianity. Our lunchtime congregation acted as a sounding board for the ideas of Part One, as we seek to reach out and touch the working community in the West End of London. My thanks to both for their encouragement and inspiration.

On a personal note I am very grateful to Elizabeth Blundell for breaking the back of the typing. I never would have got started without her. I would also like to thank Alison David for her cover design. My family, too, have had to be patient over this Christmas as I have buried myself in the depths of Wales to finish the job. It is to them that I dedicate what follows.

Kim Swithinbank
January 1988

Foreword

It was a Thursday night at All Souls – a training evening. I decided to head upstairs into the Langham Room, where Kim Swithinbank was conducting a session on evangelism. I pushed the door open and crept to the back. No one took the faintest notice of me. Ballpoints were out, the overhead projector was whirring, Kim was speaking. As I sat listening, the thought came to me – Only ten yards away the DJs of Radio One are hard at work, on the other side is a great hotel. Down the road are the stores of Europe's greatest shopping arcade, the lights of the nearby embassies are burning into the night, hospitals, colleges and banks are surrounding us here – and here in the Langham Room were the people – or at least some of them – who could be equipped to create a great network of truth and trust throughout the area.

Kim was still speaking, and I began taking notes myself. Maybe I didn't need to, because some of the things he was saying then I seem to recognise in the pages of *The Natural Touch*. There's a lot of reassurance here. Do I need a special summons to be an evangelist for God? With a ten-gallon personality and a power-boosted grip in my handshake? Kim Swithinbank doesn't seem to think so!

Come to think of it, some of the most brilliant evangelists we have around us here in London are rather new to the Christian faith themselves. They would be shocked to hear themselves described as evangelists. But they are.

I can think of students, a man from a North Sea oil rig, a

casino croupier, a speech therapist, a video-tape engineer and not a few computer analysts – all worshippers of the Lord God today. But how did it come about? What this book does, in effect, is to take us upstairs into the Langham Room, where we can hear Kim talking his head off, and enthusing into the night about the greatest of privileges – helping others to move under the leadership and Lordship of Jesus Christ.

Richard Bewes
Rector of All Souls Church
Langham Place, London W.1.

A Few Words of Introduction

'Why can't we get rid of the word "evangelism"?' So asked a questioner at a recent conference I was leading. The title of my current job is Director of Evangelism, so behind that question was the implicit threat, 'Why can't we get rid of you, Kim?' Needless to say I found it a slightly threatening question! And yet the more I thought about it, and the more I have gone on thinking about it, the more I see it is a very important question. The questioner didn't want us to stop passing on the good news. He merely thought that the word 'evangelism' was a difficult word for many Christians. Why is that?

In the first place, many Christians find 'evangelism' is a threatening word. Passing on the good news to others is difficult enough without using an off-putting word like 'evangelism' to describe it. If we talk about good news, and about passing on good news, it seems much more within our reach. After all, most of us can't keep good news to ourselves!

Penny, my wife, had some good news for me one morning some years ago. I was emerging from an important interview. She had been doing a little window-shopping and had found a ring! Together we went to look at it, and bought it. To be more precise Penny bought it as she was working and I was still an impoverished student. However, we decided to keep the good news of our engagement to ourselves as it was at least fifteen months before we could get married. The ring went in my pocket and we drove to my parents' home determined to keep our secret. We'd been home five minutes when – you've guessed it – we couldn't keep the good news to ourselves.

'Evangelism' sounds very threatening to many people. Telling people good news sounds very much more achievable – and much more fun!

'Evangelism' is also seen by many to be a technical word. When we use that word, we often think in terms of techniques. True evangelism, however, is not primarily a matter of technique. In my job, which involves encouraging people in evangelism, I do spend time teaching people how they can pass on the good news, including teaching them techniques, but that's not the heart of what we are talking about.

Furthermore, 'evangelism' sounds like an expert word. We are tempted to think that evangelism must be an expert's job and not for the ordinary Christian. I hope to show that evangelism, far from being a job for the experts, is a job for every Christian. The problem is that we live in an age of 'isms' and 'ologies' – the age of the expert. If you are discussing something in a news programme on television and you are going to have any credibility you have to introduce the expert – Professor So-and-so, or somebody else with a long string of initials after their name. Therefore we conclude that evangel*ism* must be an expert task. We must leave it to the expert. That's Kim's job, he's the Director of Evangelism. I'm not responsible, it's not my gift.

However, I think the most important reason for avoiding the word 'evangelism' is that it's not a biblical word. The equivalent to our word evangelism is not found in the New Testament. Yes, the word 'evangelism' comes from a Greek word which is used in the New Testament but that word simply means 'to announce good news'. It's not a technical word in the New Testament; it's not an expert word; it's not a threatening word; it's a joyful word. When we think of

2

it in these terms, it puts it more within the reach of most Christians; and that is exactly what I want to do.

What I want to suggest by calling this book '*The Natural Touch*' is that whenever our lives touch the lives of others something of the Christian good news should be communicated, something of Jesus and of his love for us; and it should happen naturally.

Isn't that how most of us became Christians? When I met a group of Christians and my life touched theirs I was fascinated by them. They had something. I couldn't define it. They couldn't express it very well – they hadn't done a course on evangelism; they had no techniques; you certainly wouldn't have called them experts! Yet there was something there when their lives touched mine and I came to Christ. I suspect most of us would tell a similar story.

But how can it happen in our lives? How can we develop this natural touch in evangelism? That's the subject of this book. In the first part we will look at the principles of how we can learn to build this sort of thinking and understanding of our task as Christians into our own experience – learning to make 'effective contact'. In the second part we will look at 'effective communication'. For when we begin to make effective contact with people we discover that communicating the good news to them is not simply a matter of explaining a few simple steps. They have lots of questions. We will look therefore both at how to tackle people's questions and also at some of the most common questions that are asked.

1: The Nerve Centre

Touch has to do with nerves. They are the way we actually know about touch. A message is sent along our nerves from the ends of our fingers to the nerve centre. When I was having supper recently with my Mother, she passed me my plate. I picked it up and immediately a message went through to my nerve centre saying: 'That plate's hot. Put it down!' – which I did instantly. Similarly when we communicate through touch we send a message from the nerve centre to the ends of our fingers. Coming back from holiday on an overnight train, our youngest was a bit slow getting to sleep. So I stroked her head gently, communicating, through my touch, love and a sense of security to her. There are times when I touch my children in another way seeking to communicate something rather different! However, they know by the way I touch them what is the message that is coming from my nerve centre.

Some Christians already seem to have a natural touch in passing on the good news. It may just be the look in their eyes; it could be the way they say things; but wherever they go, whoever they meet, however brief the encounter, something of Jesus Christ is communicated. But we may feel, if we're honest, that when *our* lives touch the lives of others something very different is communicated. What I want to suggest in this chapter is that the most likely reason for a problem at the nerve ends, where we touch people, is a more serious problem at the nerve centre – we are sending the wrong messages because we are not right at the centre.

We need to adjust the nerve centre in our Christian lives so that the messages we send out are the right ones – so that we begin to communicate something of Jesus and his good news whenever our lives touch the lives of others.

But what is the nerve centre of our Christian lives? In 1 Corinthians 15, Paul says that at the nerve centre of every Christian should be the gospel, the good news. He is writing this letter to a group of Corinthian Christians, some of whom were in danger of shifting their ground, the basis of their Christian faith – who were in danger, if you like, of losing the nerve centre. So he reminds them of what is of first importance.

> Now I would remind you, brethren, in what terms I preached to you the gospel, which you received, in which you stand, by which you are saved if you hold it fast, unless you believed in vain. For I delivered to you as of first importance what I also received, that Christ died for our sins (1 Corinthians 15.1–3).

and then he goes on to explain the gospel of Jesus' death and resurrection.

The good news is the key. It is 'of first importance'. But why is it so important? Paul gives three fundamental reasons for the importance of the good news not only for those Corinthians but also for us.

The Key to Our Past

First he says the good news is the key to our past. It is the good news 'which you received'. He reminds the Corinthians of how they became Christians, of how they entered into a relationship with God. It came about when he preached the gospel and they received it. That is, they became Christians when they heard and believed the good news. That is the only way into the experience of knowing God and Jesus Christ. If we are Christians, it must be because we heard and received the good nes of Jesus Christ.

It is the key to our past as Christians. There is only one way in.

Where we live in North London we have a marvellous environmental one way system, so wonderful that our road is 'no entry' at both ends! There is a way in, but it is in the middle. In fact from the main road there is only one way to drive a car to our front door. Look on a map and it looks as if there are lots of ways; but they don't work. There is only one way in. And there is only one way into the Christian life. Paul says to the Corinthians, 'How did you come to Christ? It was because you heard the gospel and you received it.'

If we look back on our own lives we will acknowledge that that is also true of us. At first as my life touched the lives of other Christians I became interested; but it was as I heard the message of the good news, as I understood it and as I received it that I became a Christian. How are our friends going to experience what we have experienced in knowing God? They too can only come in through hearing and receiving the good news.

I don't think there are many Christians who would disagree that the good news is the key to our past. The problem is that we often think of the good news just in terms of the past. Many would say that they have moved on to new things now in their Christian lives, and have left the simple gospel behind. Such a thought would be totally foreign to Paul. For him the gospel, the good news, is not only the key to our past, but also the key to our present.

The Key to Our Present

The good news is not only the good news 'which you received'; it is also the good news 'in which you stand'. Effectively, Paul says to the Corinthians: 'There's something you need to understand. Just as there was only one way for you to come into the Christian experience, so there is only one way for you to continue, only one ground on which you can stand; and that is the ground of the good news of Jesus Christ.' The barrier that prevented us entering in the first place into a relationship with God, and the obstacle which would entail our having to leave his presence immediately, if it hadn't been dealt with, are one and the same, namely our sin, our rebellion against God. The good news tells us that 'Christ died for our sins in accordance with the Scriptures;' that what prevented us coming into the presence of God was dealt with by Jesus on the cross. That good news is announced in the gospel; but it is the key not only to our past but also to our present.

It is easy for us to begin to take God's forgiveness for granted – to think 'I'm not as bad as I used to be' or 'I've given up a lot for God, I deserve to be forgiven'. Paul reminds us that the only way in which we can stand in the presence of God today is because of the good news of Jesus' death for us. We have no rights in this area. We have no other ground to stand on. Every Christian activity I engage in has its roots in the good news. I cannot pray except through Jesus Christ. My praises and the worship of my life in service of God and others will be unacceptable to God unless they are offered through Jesus Christ. I will never understand the Bible without the help of the Spirit of Christ. I cannot live the Christian life in the real world without his help either. In short the whole of my present Christian experience depends on the fact that I stand on the good news. It is the key to the present.

The Key to Our Future

The third truth that Paul brings to the attention of his Corinthian readers is that the good news is the key to the future. So Paul reminds them that this good news is not only the good news 'which you received' and the good news 'in which you stand' but it is also the good news 'by which you are saved, if you hold it fast'. This is the main point that Paul is wanting to make to the Corinthians in this passage. The tense, 'by which you are saved', is a present tense but the thought is clearly of the future, for the good news is something to which they have to hold fast as they look towards the end of their lives or to Jesus' return. The salvation that is given to us through the Christian good news is assured but not yet fully received. That's why the good news is the key to our future. It is because it assures us through Jesus' resurrection from the dead that we too will be raised and spend eternity with God.

At present we stand knowing that we are forgiven because Jesus has died for our sins in accordance with the Scriptures. That assures the past and the present. Our future is assured by his resurrection from the dead. But it was the fact of his resurrection that some of the Corinthians were doubting. If we were to read on in chapter 15 we would discover that they were shifting their ground, changing the centre of their belief. Paul warns them of the dangers involved and seeks to remind them that the good news is not an optional extra in the Christian life. It is not simply the way we become Christians. We do not grow out of it. It cannot be put on one side. We cannot pick and choose which bits of the message we will continue to believe and which we will reject. According to Paul to be a Christian is to be a 'good news' person, for our past, our present and our future all depends upon it. It is the nerve centre of our being as Christians.

What is the point of all this in the light of what we were thinking about at the beginning of this chapter? It is this. If the good news is the key to our past, present and future then it needs to be right at the nerve centre of our lives as Christians. If it is and if we see ourselves in the light of the good news, then when our lives touch the lives of others it will be the good news which is communicated. That understanding of ourselves will be the governing principle which will dictate the messages that we send out to the point of contact. Therefore we will not be able to help communicating something of that good news to others.

Paul gives us an example of this principle working out in his own life later in this same chapter, when he says 'by the grace of God, I am what I am.' This is the great apostle speaking; and yet he was aware of the fact throughout his life that he was the one who had persecuted the Church of God. So despite all that he had achieved for God, despite the hardships that he had suffered, he knew that he would never deserve God's love and forgiveness. He saw himself as a rebel but he knew that because of the good news 'by the grace of God I am what I am'. It is as if he says: 'I understand myself in the light of God's grace. I am a Christian, I am an apostle, simply by God's grace, his undeserved favour and love for me shown supremely in Jesus' death and resurrection on my behalf. What I'm telling you about the way you ought to understand yourself, that's how *I* understand *myself*. By the grace of God I am what I am.'

But look at the result! Paul goes on: 'His grace to me was not in vain. On the contrary, I worked harder than any of them.' Harder at what? Harder at the task of sharing the good news. The effect of Paul's understanding himself in this way was that it drove him out to share that good news with others. Once he understood what God had done for him it became central to his whole understanding of himself. He had to communicate that message to others.

We have a retired missionary on the staff of our church. Everyone she comes across is touched with the gospel. Whenever you talk to her you find she has been talking to people about Jesus. It's no big deal to her – it's as natural as breathing. Yet to most of us it's quite extraordinary. She just has this ability so that whoever she touches is touched with Christ.

As you get to know her you discover it's because the gospel is central to her whole understanding of herself. She is still thrilled after thirty or forty years with the fact that Jesus died for her, that he loves her and that he rose again to assure her of her future salvation. When she hears a talk on the good news, she's not thinking about how she would have put it better or about how she's heard it so many times before and why doesn't the preacher introduce a bit of variety. It still thrills her heart. She is full of the good news and so when her life touches the lives of others that is what is communicated.

Isn't that why young Christians are often the keenest to share the good news? For a young Christian who has just discovered what it is to know Christ personally it's terrific news. Often they don't know what they are doing; they have no technique; they aren't experts; and yet whoever they touch they touch with the gospel and they touch with Jesus Christ. The sad thing is that many of us who have been Christians longer have lost that sense of wonder. Some of us take the good news for granted. Others seem no longer to believe that it can be true for us. Maybe we've been Christians for a while but we feel we have let God down and we no longer believe that he can forgive us. It could be something specific that we have done or it may just be a sense of being a failure as a Christian in many different areas of our lives. Yet for whatever cause we no longer really accept the good news personally, or see ourselves in the light of that good news, deep down within our own being. We no longer believe that God really loves us and that the forgiveness he offers covers all sin.

If either of these things is so, then we won't have any enthusiasm for passing on the good news. So when an enthusiastic evangelist comes along and says 'Come on; all those people out there – they need to hear about Jesus. If you don't do it nobody else is going to do it!', we think 'Oh no, someone has put another burden on me. Something else I've got to do. I've got to pray. I've got to go to church; and now I've got to do evangelism.' It seems like one more burden, the straw that broke the camel's back, and we can't face it.

The message of this chapter and of this book is not that you must do evangelism. I'm not saying that. The message for all of us is clear, for me as much as for you. We need to get the nerve centre right. We need to see again that all that really matters about us can be expressed in terms of the good news. The most significant event in my past was when I received the good news. The most important thing about me now is that I am standing on the truth of the good news, that Jesus died for me. The most important thing about my future is that I am looking forward to a resurrection to be with God; and I am assured of that because of the good news, because Jesus rose from the dead. In short we need to see that we are 'good news' people; and if we see ourselves in those terms then that is what we will communicate to others as well.

I am, as you already know, a married man. Any one who knows me even remotely well knows that. I also have three children. If someone were to meet me casually in the street they might not know these things; but if I get to know someone at all well, they soon find out. Why? Because my wife and family are a central part of my life. If someone wants to know me, then they will have to learn something about my family as well. In the same way, only more so, the good news is central to our lives as Christians, says Paul. If we understand that to be true then, when people get to know us, they will get to know the good news as well. Probably not all at once; but naturally, over a period of time, as they get to know us better.

We will not all communicate it in the same way; but if we see ourselves as 'good news' people, something of the good news will be communicated in every relationship we form. When you meet some people, the first thing they do is produce their wallet and show you a picture of their family. Personally that's not my style, but to some people it's the natural thing. So too some people can talk about their faith easily and naturally at a first meeting; whereas for others it takes longer. The manner and the timing matter very little. What matters is that we have the nerve centre right so that we see how central the good news is to our lives. If that is so, the manner and the timing will largely look after themselves.

The problem for many of us is that the good news is not central to our thinking about ourselves. Therefore when it is suggested that we should 'do evangelism' it seems as if someone is asking us to do something which is foreign to our nature. 'Evangelism', if I may be permitted to use that word again, is seen by us as an add-on, an eccentric hobby that amuses some Christians. However if we see ourselves as 'good news' people, and if that good news is central to our lives, then if people get to know us at all well they must get to know something of the good news too. It doesn't matter whether we call it evangelism or not – as I explained in the introduction I think it may well be better to forget the word. What's important is that we understand what really matters about our lives and that we let others catch a glimpse of that as they get to know us better.

When we see how central the good news is to our own Christian lives, when we see afresh how much God loves us, how wonderful it is to be forgiven, then we will want to share the good news. We'll have the equivalent of that little ring in a box. We'll think of Jesus and we won't be able to keep the good news to ourselves because we will be so excited and thrilled by it. No-one will need to tell us to do evangelism but when our lives touch the lives of others, whether it be a colleague at work, or the person from whom we buy our newspaper, whether it be members of our family, or a neighbour at home, however permanent or however transitory that touch may be, something of Jesus Christ will be communicated. That's what we are aiming for. That's the natural touch.

2: The Power Source

There is another important characteristic that this touch displays: not only is it natural, it is also powerful. People with this touch seem to have an electricity about them. You may have experienced the tingle of static electricity – perhaps when a shop has a new carpet, and you touch the chrome handrail; or perhaps when you open a car door. People who have a natural touch with the good news seem to have a similar effect. Not only is it a natural touch but it is a powerful touch; some sort of spark seems to jump across from them to others as their lives touch.

This power is something that most of us long for if we have already developed a desire to pass on the Christian good news. For if we have that desire, if we see the need of those who've not yet heard of Jesus Christ and if we're thrilled ourselves by the message of the good news, then we have a longing for the power to be able to communicate it effectively. For the task of communicating that news seems so daunting. If we look at the world which needs to hear about Jesus Christ, if we look at one city, if we look even at our neighbourhood or our workplace or home, we feel small and the task seems enormous. In light of the enormity of the task of reaching the world for Christ we feel daunted, weak and helpless and therefore we long, naturally, for power.

Not surprisingly therefore there is a demand for power in the Church today; and where there is a demand someone will propose a source of supply. It's the law of the market place but it works in the Church as well. There is a great deal of power teaching in the Church today, some of which has been very helpful, some of which has led to a great deal of confusion and to some false expectations amongst Christians. The important questions for us in the context of the subject we are concerned with are 'Where is power to be found for the task of communicating the good news of Jesus? What is the power source?'

We're going to look again at the example of Paul and at the secret of his power. I hope that as a result we will see the same demonstration of the Spirit and of power that he speaks of as we seek to take the good news to others. I hope too that we will form right expectations of what it means to see God's power at work and that we will develop the right approach to finding his source of power.

Paul is writing to the same Corinthian Christians, but this time he is talking about his experience of bringing the gospel to them:

> When I came to you, brethren, I did not come proclaiming to you the testimony of God in lofty words or wisdom. For I decided to know nothing among you except Jesus Christ and him crucified. And I was with you in weakness and much fear and trembling; and my speech and my message were not in plausible words of wisdom, but in demonstration of the Spirit and of power, that your faith might not rest in the wisdom of men but in the power of God (1 Corinthians 2.1–5).

A Feeling of Weakness

Two things stand out in these years. The first is that Paul had a feeling of great weakness. He says to them 'I was with you in weakness and much fear and trembling'. Isn't that a strange thing for the great apostle Paul to write? The man who, after Jesus Christ, probably had more of an impact for the Christian good news on the world than any other single man who has ever lived. And yet he says here 'I was with you in weakness and much fear and trembling'. Was there something perhaps rather frightening about the Corinthians? Were they very intellectual people who he thought might tear him to shreds? Were they particularly aggressive in their reaction to Paul? What was it that caused this fear?

There is no evidence that it was any of those things, for this is not an isolated comment of Paul's. He seems to make this point about his own weakness again and again in his writings. He says on another occasion that God has put the treasure of the gospel message in earthen vessels or in jars of clay. It seems that Paul felt it to be a principle that God has chosen to show his power through our weakness. The reason for that is shown in our passage here. At the end Paul says that the purpose of his feelings of weakness was 'that your faith might not rest in the wisdom of men but in the power of God'.

This reasoning contrasts with much of our thinking in the Church today. The question that many are asking is this. 'If we are to be representatives of a powerful God, if we are to be those who are preaching the Kingdom of God, the Kingdom of God's power, how can we do that if we are weak and fearful and fallible human beings?' For most of us, frankly, the very thought of talking to our friends about Jesus Christ makes us feel weak at the knees. So we think to ourselves 'If I'm so weak, how can I represent a God of power?' But the question misses the point. Paul's point is this. If I'm a powerful person and if I have a feeling of power, then when people respond to the message that I speak they may get confused. They may think that the change that has taken place in their lives is because of something to do with me and my power. Conversely, if I'm a weak person and I can be seen to be a fallible and ordinary human being, then when I preach this message to them, when they hear it and respond to it and their lives are changed, they will know that I cannot possibly have brought about that change in their lives, that it must be God and his power that has been at work.

There are two common ways of making a point, by

similarity or by contrast. Imagine, for instance, that we are wanting to demonstrate the strength of the world's strongest man. We could show his picture pulling Concorde along with his own bare arms alongside a picture of Concorde being towed by a powerful truck or lorry. Our picture would then say 'Look at this man, he's as strong as this lorry' – a picture of similarity. Alternatively we could take a picture of the man alongside the archetypal seven stone weakling and say 'Look at this man and his strength in comparison to this man and his weakness.' Both would make the same point but in a different way.

The New Testament teaches us that God chooses to show his power not by making us powerful but by keeping us weak and showing his power in contrast to our weakness. In the previous chapter Paul reminded the Corinthians that they were living proof that 'God chose what is foolish in the world to shame the wise. God chose what is weak in the world to shame the strong.' That is the way God has chosen to do it; and his reason for doing that is so that there can be no possible confusion as to where the power comes from. Therefore we should expect to feel weak just as Paul did.

This may at first seem a depressing thought, but I find great encouragement here. It means this feeling of weakness which, frankly, I suspect we all experience in seeking to pass on the good news to others, is not something that will prevent us from being used by God in the work of the good news. In fact it is actually an essential qualification for being used by God and for his power being passed through us. Do you feel weak at the thought of inviting a friend to come along and hear the message of the good news at a guest service? Do you feel weak at the thought of talking about Jesus Christ with your friends? That's a good sign. It's normal Christian experience and it's necessary if God is to use us in this task.

A Demonstration of Power

But that's not the whole story; Paul also saw and experienced a demonstration of God's power. For he goes

17

on to say that his speech and his message were not in plausible words of wisdom but in demonstration of the Spirit and of power. By the way he phrases this it's clear that this was not a separate experience – not that he felt weak to start with and then felt powerful but, rather, that at one and the same time he had a feeling of weakness but saw a demonstration of the Spirit and of power.

What was this demonstration? If we read Paul's letters to the Corinthians it is quite clear that he did perform a number of miracles amongst them and that they did see, as he calls them, 'the signs of an apostle' working amongst them. However, it seems that in these opening two chapters of 1 Corinthians when Paul talks about the demonstration of the Spirit and power that's not what he has in mind. In this context, it seems that power is associated with God's saving message. So in verse 18 of chapter 1 we read that 'the word of the cross (Paul's message) is folly to those who are perishing but to us who are being saved it is the power of God'. That power has to do with the message which brings salvation.

Similarly when he talks about the work of the Spirit in chapter 2, he is not seen as the worker of miracles, which he is in some other contexts, but his work is associated here with revelation. He is the one who teaches the truth, which is the New Testament's more normal understanding of the work of the Spirit. The Spirit is seen in these chapters as the one who can show us the mind of God. So in chapter 2 verse 10 Paul writes 'God has revealed these things to us through the Spirit. For the Spirit searches everything even the depths of God.' Therefore it would seem natural to take the demonstration of the Spirit and of power here to be that what was 'folly to the Greeks and a stumbling block to Jews' was understood and accepted by the Corinthians. For that process of people coming from unbelief to faith can only happen as their minds are opened by the Spirit and as their wills are given the power to change direction by the Spirit. That seems to be what Paul has in mind here when he speaks about a demonstration of the Spirit and of power.

Now of course if a physical miracle takes place – the healing of someone with cancer, for example – it is easy to see that that is a demonstration of the Spirit and of power. However, from our viewpoint, when someone comes to faith in Jesus Christ it is not so immediately obvious – there is nothing that we can see; but in New Testament terms it is just as much, if not more, a demonstration of the Spirit and of power. Though God surely can and does work in the physical realm today the New Testament is clear that he doesn't always do so; and from what we experience today, it's quite clear that he doesn't always do so. Even those who claim healing gifts in the Church today have nowhere near a hundred per cent record. So we must conclude that God doesn't always heal but that he does always work his power through the message of the cross which Paul spoke.

Joni Eareckson, author of *Joni* and *A Step Further*, had a tragic accident when she was seventeen, diving into shallow water and breaking her neck. She is now paralysed from the neck downwards. Many many people have told her that God wants to heal her, and have sought to bring her healing. She, as she writes very honestly and openly, has tried to open herself up to that but God has not healed her. Why not? What is God's purpose? I don't know God's particular purpose for Joni but I can see in her life this same principle of power in weakness being worked out. For in her weakness I can think of few people in the Church today who have been more used by God than someone like Joni. She has this natural touch, this touch of power. There is something about her which is quite remarkable: through her struggles God seems to work in a demonstration of the Spirit and of power.

Max Sinclair (who wrote *Halfway to Heaven*) had a similar experience when he was in a car crash about ten years ago. At first he was completely paralysed from the neck downwards and then, amazingly, in answer to prayer, he began to get better, much against the expectations of the doctors. He thought for a time that he was going to get fully well but then the process stopped halfway. He can walk now but he walks with a limp. He can write but only with his left hand; his right hand is still largely useless. He is paralysed almost completely down one side. Max has had to cope with that and still has, I know, tremendous feelings of frustration and of weakness. Yet through his writing and speaking and also through his other ministry Max has this same touch when he touches people with Jesus; for though he feels weak God's power is demonstrated in the lives of those he touches.

It's important for us to have right expectations about how God is going to demonstrate his power. We must expect that we are still going to feel weak even when his power is at work. We must learn to see beneath the surface and recognise God's power when we see it. Think for a moment of your group of friends, at work or at college or at home, your non-Christian friends. Think of the person who you feel is least likely to become a Christian. Imagine them in your mind. There they are, probably very resistant to the good news though you've mentioned Christianity to them once or twice and met with a pretty stony silence, even outright opposition. Consider for a moment if they were to turn from the way they are living now, to turn right round, and come to faith in Jesus Christ. Can you think of a greater example of a demonstration of God's Spirit and God's power? We're amazed by the physical miracles, because they don't happen very often, they seem very exciting to us; but the really important miracle is the one God works in the heart and the will when people turn from living for themselves to live for him. A friend of my brother's who was at medical school with him was really antagonistic to the Christian Union. On one occasion when the CU were having a barbecue on the lawn outside the hall of residence he decided that they didn't deserve to enjoy themselves. So he made a few flour bombs, went up towards the top of the block and proceeded to deposit them from a great height on the CU below. That was fairly typical of his attitude to the CU. He couldn't stand them; he hated Christians; and yet just a few months later his life was turned round and he began to follow Jesus Christ. Now to everybody in the college that was a clear demonstration of God's Spirit and God's power.

The Power Source

The final question for this chapter is to discover the source of this power. How can we, even if we are going to feel weak, make sure that we see this demonstration of the Spirit and of power in the lives of our friends? Where does it come from? What is the power source? Clearly this power is God's power, for all power comes from him. Furthermore all God's power demonstrated in the world today is worked by his Spirit. Therefore it must be the power of the Spirit of which Paul speaks when he refers to 'a demonstration of the Spirit and of power'.

However, that doesn't answer the question of how we can see this power at work as we seek to pass on the good news to others. What did Paul consider to be the secret of this 'demonstration of the Spirit and of power?' In these opening two chapters of 1 Corinthians power seems to be very closely linked with Paul's message. As we have already seen, in Paul's view, 'the word of the cross is folly to those who are perishing but to us who are being saved it is the power of God.' What is the power of God? It is the message of the cross, the good news. Paul makes a similar point in his letter to the Romans when he says that 'the gospel is the power of God unto salvation' (Romans 1.16). If we ask the question, therefore, 'Where does Paul's power come from?', his answer is that it comes from his message. 'The secret of my power', says Paul, 'is that I preach the gospel, the message of Jesus and him crucified.'

In the Church we are often in danger of dividing the power of God – we talk about the power of the Spirit as if it were separate from the power of God or the power of Jesus. Furthermore we separate the Spirit from the power of the Word. There is a saying: 'If you have the Word without the Spirit you dry up as a Christian; if you have the Spirit without the Word you blow up as a Christian; but if you have the

21

Spirit and the Word together you grow up as a Christian.' In some ways that's quite helpful; but in other ways it isn't, because the first two are simply not possible. You cannot have the Word of God apart from the Spirit of God; for who is the Spirit of God? The Spirit of God is God's breath (the word for breath and Spirit in both Hebrew and Greek are the same); and breath is essential to speech. We can't talk without breathing. If you try talking without breathing at the same time there will be no sound. Similarly God speaks by his Spirit, his breath. Therefore the Word of God always comes by the Spirit of God. Wherever the Word of God is, the Spirit of God is there also. So Jesus says of his own words 'My words are Spirit and Life'.

All these are tied together. We cannot separate them. There are those in the Church today who want to have the power of God, the power of the Spirit, but they put their Bibles down. They look for power in order to reach others for Christ but they look beyond the good news itself. But we'll never find that power unless we find it through God's Word and through the gospel. That's the way in which God shows his power. So what was the secret of Paul's power? It was that he decided to commit himself to the word of the gospel. In the verses I quoted at the beginning of this chapter Paul says 'I decided to know nothing among you except Jesus Christ and him crucified'. That was the key decision. That was the secret of his power; and if we want to see a similar demonstration of the Spirit and of power in the lives of our friends we need to make a similar decision.

We may feel that to talk about Jesus and about his crucifixion to our friends would be impossible. We may feel that the clever people we know, like the Greeks, would think we were just plain stupid or foolish for speaking about such a message; and that our religious friends, like the Jews, would find it a stumbling block as we explained that they can't get to heaven on their own good deeds but need to come and recognise that they need the death of Jesus and the forgiveness that that secures. But the message of these verses and of the New Testament as a whole is that, if we want to see a demonstration of God's power by his Spirit, then we too must decide to know nothing except Jesus Christ and him crucified. That doesn't mean that we talk about Jesus and the cross all the time – so, we arrrive at work on Monday morning and someone says 'Had a good weekend?' and we say 'Yes, I was learning about Jesus and his cross' at the very first opportunity. Nor does it mean that every time they start talking about the weather, we say we would rather talk about Jesus and him crucified. It couldn't possibly mean that. We would just get written off as cranks and loonies very very quickly, and probably for good reason. But it does mean that when opportunities do arise, and they do and will arise if we look for them and ask God to provide them, we will seek to speak about Jesus and about his cross; that'll be the message we are trying to put across.

That may sound obvious but it is in sharp contrast to the message that we often put across. For often when opportunities arise we talk about ourselves and our own experience; or we talk about our youth group or our church. Not that I'm saying we shouldn't talk about our own experience of God or about our churches. What I am saying is that if we stop there and don't go beyond that and begin to speak about Jesus, we will never see the demonstration of the Spirit and of power; because the power doesn't lie in talking about my experience of Jesus or in talking about our church or Christian group. Those are very useful ways of leading in to talking about Jesus; but the power comes when we speak about Jesus and him crucified. For God has chosen to reveal his power in this extraordinary message.

It is a paradox that the power of God is shown when we speak about a man who was strung up on a cross in utter helplessness and weakness, unable to move his hands or his feet because of the nails that held him. Yet paradoxical as it may be, it is this message which is the power source. If we want to see a demonstration of the Spirit's power in the lives of our friends who are not yet Christians then we need look no further. Much time and emotional energy is being wasted in the Church today in the pursuit of power in order to reach the world for Christ; yet all the while the power is right in front of us. It comes from God; all power does. It is demonstrated by his Spirit, God's agent in the world today. But it is found in the message of the good news itself. We need never ask again 'Where will I get the power I need in order to reach my friends for Christ?' Instead, in simple obedience, we need to take the message of the good news to the world, feeling very weak in ourselves, sensing the enormity of the task, yet knowing that the message we bear is not only the answer to the world's deepest needs, but that it is also the source of the power that we lack.

3: Everybody's Doing it

'It's not my responsibility, it's somebody else's job!' I expect
we have all said that ourselves on occasions; or at least we have
all heard people say it. Effectively that's what the British
Telecom engineer said to me the day when I went to ask him
why all three of the phones coming into our house were not
working at the same time (two of the phones were used by my
wife who was running a business from home at the time). He
was fiddling round with the wires by the road outside our
house and I wondered if there was perhaps some link between
his activity and our problem. This suspicion grew when our
next door neighbour's phone was also disconnected; and it
hardened when our neighbour's phone started ringing in
response to our number! However he was adamant; his was
purely a routine rewiring job, part of the modernisation of the
network; 'No, that's not my responsibility. I'm just renewing
the wiring. It's a general thing, it's got nothing particularly to
do with your house; that's somebody else's job. You'll have to
ring the exchange.'

'It's not my responsibility, it's somebody else's job.' That
kind of thinking is not peculiar to British Telecom nor even
to the world of work; and though it may occasionally be
frustrating, especially when it's your phone that's not
working, it is only fair that we have to think in that way
about jobs. If everybody took responsibility within their
own companies or firms for everything, there would be
utter chaos and we would be submerged under a burden of
work. It would be quite unbearable. The same truth has

been rediscovered in the Church. We now recognise that different people have different gifts and abilities. This has been enormously beneficial to the Church, perhaps especially to those of us who have an 'up-front' ministry. Now it is clearly recognised that we are not necessarily good at everything! Most of us, for instance, are hopeless at administration. Before, we were expected to do everything; now it is realised that we can't, and shouldn't be doing everything. Some of us aren't very good at leading singing; we find other people are better at that. Some people are very good at leading small groups, others at caring for people or helping them through difficulties.

The problem begins when we apply this sort of thinking to the work of spreading the good news. We think to ourselves 'Evangelism, not my responsibility; that's somebody else's job.' After all, doesn't the Bible talk about evangelists? It's one of the gifts, isn't it? But not mine. Therefore it must be somebody else's and not my responsibility. In the immortal parody of the words of Isaiah, we say 'Lord, here am I. Please send somebody else!'

However, even if we do see ourselves as having some responsibility for passing on the good news, we see it in limited terms. I don't know how much you know about American football, but they do everything bigger and better in the States. So they don't just have one team in the way we have, with both attackers and defenders on the field at the same time. Instead they have two teams. When they're attacking they have one team on the field (called the offence, pronounced off-fence). When they are defending they have a different team on the field (called the defence, pronounced dee-fence). They come on when the others go off and vice versa. Many of us think about the work of the good news in that way.

We consider people like Billy Graham and Luis Palau as being on the offence team. Their job is to go out and look for opportunities. But we say of ourselves 'I'm on the defence team. If someone asks me why I am a Christian, I tell them; but I am not actually going to go out and look for any opportunities.' That was certainly how I saw things in my early Christian life. The first three or four years I was a Christian I thought that my job was to defend God. So when my school friends attacked God, I would defend him, hold up my end. But when it came to looking for opportunities, or seeking to take the good news out to the people in the school who didn't yet know about it, I didn't see that was my job. But I came to see that it was.

That lesson is one we all need to learn from the New Testament. We need to rediscover the New Testament pattern, not only for the use of gifts, but also for the work of the good news. That pattern seems to involve all of us, in some way, in going out not just as part of the defence team but on the offence team as well. That's the pattern we see in Acts 8 amongst those who were scattered at the start of the first great persecution of the Church. There they were after the stoning of Stephen. Jesus had given them the plan for the growth of the Church – they were to begin in Jerusalem and then they were to spread out, first to Judea and Samaria, and then to the ends of the earth. In Acts 8 they find themselves for the first time forced out beyond Jerusalem. They are scattered throughout the region of Judea and Samaria.

The interesting point to note from Luke's account, however, concerns what they did when they were scattered. He writes that 'those who were scattered went about preaching the Word' (Acts 8.4). It is this group that I want to concentrate on, and ask two simple questions about them.

First of all, who were they? Who were those who were scattered? In many ways we don't know who they were, though we know one of them was called Philip because he is mentioned later. But we do know who they weren't. Luke tells us that 'they were all scattered throughout the region of Judea and Samaria, except the apostles' (Acts 8.1). For the first time the good news gets beyond Jerusalem to the region of Judea and Samaria; but who takes the message? Answer, not the apostles but the ordinary Christians who were scattered. A few years ago there was a popular comedy show entitled *Not the Nine O'Clock News*. Here in a way we have the story of 'Not the Apostles', not the experts. It's the way God seems to have chosen to take the good news beyond Jerusalem to the region of Judea and Samaria. Who did he choose for this strategic first stage of the task of taking the good news to the world at large? He chose the ordinary Christians.

We need to be careful, however, before saying that because God chose to act in this way on that particular occasion, he will necessarily always act in the same way. Special care needs to be taken when interpreting the book of Acts and other narrative passages of the New Testament, because sometimes there are special reasons why particular things happen. We cannot assume that the same things apply today. Sometimes they do, sometimes they don't. We need to ask the question whether this is an example of a general principle or an example of a special case. Perhaps, for instance, the apostles were unable to go. Maybe they had got other engagements at that time and therefore they had to send the ordinary Christians as a special case. Now that may sound unlikely, but there could have been some special reason.

However, if we look at the rest of the New Testament and ask whether this story is a typical case or a special case, we find it must be typical. This seems to have been the normal way in which the good news was spread in New Testament times. So, for example, Peter writing to ordinary Christians in 1 Peter tells them that they should all be able to give a reason for the hope that was in them. When we think further, for a moment, about how the churches grew, using our powers of deduction, we must conclude that the early expansion of the Church was largely the work of the ordinary Christians. The apostles had a strategic role to play but they could never have achieved the phenomenal growth of the early Church on their own.

Think of the church in Northern Greece, for example. Paul spent just a short time there, yet when he writes to

28

them, it is quite clear from his letters that those Christians have not only expanded to form a decent-sized church but that the message has gone forth from them into the whole region. He only went to Thessalonica. But from those Christians the message had spread out into the whole surrounding area. Similarly in Asia Minor (modern Turkey) Paul seems to have chosen to concentrate his evangelistic thrust in Ephesus, spending two or three years there. His reason appears to have been that Ephesus was the hub of that part of the world. Traders, sailors, officials serving the whole area had to pass through Ephesus. He could rely on them once they were converted and established to take the good news to the inland areas. That is presumably how the good news reached many of the early Christians.

There is, however, a more important reason for believing that the task of passing on the good news is the responsibility of every Christian. As Christians our primary calling is to become more like God – 'to be conformed to the likeness of his Son' as Paul puts it in Romans 8. Now if we look at the character of God, we see that he is, amongst other things, a missionary God, that his heart burns with the love that reaches out into the world. In Genesis 3 we see Adam and Eve, after their rebellion, hiding from God; but what does God do? He comes and looks for them in the garden and he says to them 'Where are you?'. That is what God is like. He looks for the lost. In the same vein Jesus said of himself when talking to Zaccheus 'The Son of Man came to seek and to save the lost'. That is the character of God.

If we look at the Holy Spirit and his work in the book of Acts we see again and again that he is pushing the Church out. He sets aside Saul and Barnabas for the work of mission. He tells Paul in a vision that he's got stuck in Asia Minor and it's time he took the gospel to Greece. Again and again the Holy Spirit is leading them into the work of mission. Not only does he lead them but he also gives them boldness. It's a familiar refrain in the book of Acts after church prayer meetings that they were all filled with the Holy Spirit who caused them to speak the word of God with boldness. Why? Because the Holy Spirit is a missionary spirit. That is what God is like.

Therefore if our primary calling is to be like God, it must include being like God in his concern for the lost. Yet there are many Christians who would claim a close personal relationship with God but who have no heart for reaching others for Christ. But surely if we are close to God then our hearts and minds will be increasingly in tune with his. So if his heart burns with love for his lost world, so should ours. If it doesn't, then perhaps we need to re-examine our relationship with God. Maybe our claims are exaggerated. Perhaps they are based more on our feelings than on reality. For a concern for the lost is as good a barometer as any of our overall spiritual well-being.

Now if we add to those biblical reasons the obvious practical reasons, then the case is unanswerable. We need to ask, for instance, 'How many Christians are there in my place of work or where I live? Who is going to reach these people with the good news of Jesus Christ if I don't? What about the street where I live at home, my block of flats? Who is going to reach the people who live there if I don't?' The task of taking the good news to the world must be our task, all of ours together. Otherwise it will never get done. We cannot leave it to the experts.

Someone may well ask 'Who then are the evangelists that the Bible speaks about?' The word only comes three times in the New Testament, once concerning Philip who is referred to as Philip the evangelist, once in a list of gifts in Ephesians 4 where Paul says that 'some are apostles, some prophets, some evangelists and some pastors and teachers', and once when Timothy is told to 'do the work of an evangelist'. It is difficult to construct a precise understanding of the New Testament view of an evangelist from these three brief references. There is some clue in the second reference that the evangelist stands between the apostles and prophets, who in Ephesians are those to whom the original gospel was given, and the pastors and teachers who care for the church. The evangelists stand between those two in some way, presumably as those who take the message that was delivered to the apostles and prophets to the world. From the other two references we can conclude little more than than Philip was an evangelist, that Timothy probably wasn't, but that he had to do the work of an evangelist anyway!

However, we can draw at least two tentative conclusions from the three references together – first, that some do have a special gift as 'evangelists'. We think naturally in terms of Billy Graham and Luis Palau and others who seem to have a special gift in this area. People like that are clearly evangelists right to the bottom of their boots. They can't do anything else. It is the only thing they are happy doing. All day, every day, they want to do evangelism. Some people seem to have that gift and we conclude that they are evangelists. That must be fair comment. However we cannot conclude that therefore we are free from any responsibility with regard to the good news. No, it would seem that the second thing that we must conclude from these references is that others of us are called to do the work, even if we are not particularly gifted as evangelists. That is certainly how I would think of myself. I see myself much more like Timothy with God saying to me 'Kim, you're a pastor and a teacher but you must do the work of an evangelist'. I can't conclude it is somebody else's job.

That becomes even clearer when we ask the second question about this group of people who were scattered. We have looked at who they were. They were the ordinary Christians and not the apostles. The second question is 'What did they do?' Before I answer that I want to ask you two questions. First, do you consider yourself in any sense to be an evangelist? Second, do you think of yourself as being called by your life and by what you say to be a witness to Jesus Christ? My guess is that most will answer 'No' to the first question and 'Yes' to the second. That was certainly the response when I asked for a show of hands in church recently. A handful answered 'Yes' to the first question, but just about every hand in the building was raised when I asked the second.

Imagine their surprise therefore when I went on to say that in New Testament terms none of us is a witness and all of us are in some measure called to be evangelists. By that I mean that in the sense that you could call Lenin 'the Commun*ist*' or 'one of the great commun*ists*' so there are few 'evangel*ists*'. But in the sense that everyone who practices commun*ism* is a commun*ist*, so too all of us are called to do the work of evangel*ism* and can therefore be accurately described as evangel*ists*.

To see the relevance of this we must return to the group who were scattered. What did these people do? The answer is not clear in the English translations. In English it says simply that they went about preaching the Word. However the word there translated 'preaching the Word' is the word from which our word 'evangelism' comes. Literally, it means they went around announcing the good news. They spoke, and they spoke about Jesus; for the good news is about Jesus. So, on another occasion when Luke mentions this same group again, he says they went about 'preaching the Lord Jesus'. Again the same word is used. They went around 'announcing the good news the Lord Jesus' – that is the literal translation of the Greek, because the good news is the Lord Jesus. They went about talking; they went about talking about Jesus.

Now why is that so important? We come back to what we were thinking about at the beginning of the chapter, about us seeing ourselves as being on the defence team (to use the American Football analogy again). We see ourselves in defensive terms, thinking of ourselves as witnesses. Our role, therefore, is to live the Christian life – that's how we see it. With the result that if someone asks us, after seeing the witness of our life, why we are the way we are, we can bear witness to God's work in our lives. The initiative is theirs. Our role is passive or defensive. So one of the most common words for describing the work of the good news in the Church today is the term 'witnessing'. Don't you talk about that in your church? It is part of our 'in' jargon. Now, don't get me wrong, living the Christian life and speaking about what God has done for us are valuable and important things to do. In fact the first is so important that a whole chapter is given over later to the importance of living the Christian life in terms of communicating the good news.

For the moment, though, we need to understand what our role is meant to be in the light of the New Testament. In those terms the life we live, and speaking about our own experience of God, are only part of what we are meant to be doing. We need to realise that in New Testament terms none of us is or ever could be a witness but that all of us are called to be those who announce the good news, who talk about Jesus. We come back to the assertion I was making earlier; for in the New Testament the word 'witness' is a very specialised word. It is used exclusively of those who were eye-witnesses of the Resurrection. They are the witnesses; they are the ones who give testimony (in Greek it is the same word). Nobody else did, nobody else could. We cannot testify to something we haven't seen. If you are not a witness to a crime, you are not called to the Old Bailey to give evidence. If you didn't witness it, you're no use in making a case.

There is a good example of this distinction between the role of the apostles in bearing witness and that of the ordinary Christians in announcing the good news in Acts 4. We pick up the story at the end of one of those famous prayer meetings in the early chapters of Acts. Luke tells us 'When they prayed, the place in which they were gathered together was shaken and they were all filled with the Holy Spirit.' With what result? 'They spoke the word of God with boldness.' Luke is speaking there about all of the Christians. But then a few verses later we read that 'with great power the *apostles* gave their *testimony* to the Resurrection of the Lord Jesus'. In the book of Acts everybody speaks the word of God; everybody can announce the good news; but only the apostles can bear witness or give testimony, because they were the ones to whom Jesus appeared after his death and resurrection. They, and only they, were the witnesses of those events; but the good news, based on their testimony, was announced by all.

You may think I am arguing over words. I hope I'm not; for this distinction has two important lessons for us before we move on. First we learn from these early Christians that all of us are called to speak the good news; not necessarily to big crowds – very few of us will be called to that; not necessarily preaching on street corners or knocking on doors; but simply to the people whom our lives naturally touch. So that these people are touched by the good news, not only by the way we live but also by what we say because, as the opportunities arise, we talk about Jesus.

That is the second thing that we need to learn from these early Christians – that what we talk about must be the Jesus of history, not primarily the Jesus of my experience. For the good news is about what God has done in and through the Jesus of history and through his death and resurrection. For though we may also speak of what God has done for us, we will want to go beyond that and say that we know that Christianity is true and not a figment of our imagination because there is hard evidence for it. That evidence does not constitute a scientific proof but it is historical evidence of the highest order. It is based on the testimony of reliable men. Their witness would stand up in a court of law. It is not based on our witness, it is based on the apostles' witness. This is particularly important when we face the criticism that Christianity works for some people but not for others. In our relativistic age this is a common statement: 'It's true for you; but it's not true for me.' We, however, are wanting to say much more than that; but if our only argument is 'This is what Jesus has done for me', then we leave ourselves wide open to the criticism and we have no answer to it. Unless we can show reasons for believing which are not just subjective (concerning our own experience), but which are objective and open to scrutiny, then we cannot complain if people write off our faith as insubstantial wishful thinking.

More than that, not only are we leaving ourselves wide open to criticism if our gospel is purely a gospel of experience, we are also denying ourselves the source of God's power for the work we are trying to do. For as we saw in the last chapter the gospel is itself God's power for salvation; and the New Testament gospel is the gospel concerning God's Son, Jesus – the Jesus who died and who rose, the Jesus who has ascended to heaven and is now seated in the position of authority at God's right hand, the Jesus before whom we will all appear one day when he returns to judge the world.

However, our words are equally empty if they concern a figure of history who has no relevance in our lives today. We want to say that today we can all know the living Lord Jesus Christ; and the reason we can be sure of that, even when we don't feel it, is because it is solidly based on the witness of reliable people, whose testimony, if you were to put them up in the Old Bailey in front of a judge and jury, would bear up to close examination. Their task was to bear witness in their day to what they had seen and heard and to record their testimony for future generations. Our task, like that of the early Christians who were scattered through Judea and Samaria, is to take the good news of that Jesus, to whom the apostles bear witness, to the people amongst whom we are scattered. Most of us aren't theological or evangelistic experts – nor were they; but they were effective. We too will be effective in God's plan for the world he loves if we will only recognise and act upon our responsibility to take the good news, not necessarily to the ends of the earth, but to those whose lives we touch.

4: Making Contact

We have been thinking so far about developing a natural touch so that, when our lives touch the lives of others, something of the good news of Jesus Christ will be communicated. We thought first of the importance of getting the nerve centre right so that at the heart of our own being we understand that as Christians our present, our past and our future all depend on the good news of Jesus Christ. We looked then at the importance of that message, not only as being the grounds on which we are Christians, but also as the power which God uses by his Spirit to change people's lives in the world today. That message of Jesus Christ and him crucified is the power source. It makes our touch not only a natural touch but also a powerful touch. In the last chapter we saw that this work of reaching out to touch others with the good news of Jesus Christ is not just the job of the experts in the Church. It is everybody's task.

The problem that many Christians have in reaching out to touch the world with the good news of Jesus Christ is that we can't touch what we can't reach. The other day our youngest, aged four, was trying to get hold of the vitamin pills which our children have every morning in the winter. She was standing by the kitchen sink and they were on the ledge behind. As she reached out with her little hand she couldn't reach and therefore she couldn't touch. Many of us as Christians cannot, in any meaningful way, touch the lives of non-Christians because we put ourselves out of reach.

Many of us are simply out of touch, out of contact, with those who don't yet know Jesus Christ.

There are two main reasons for this; the first is that if we have been Christians for some time, most if not all of our close friends are probably also Christians. Therefore the people we spend time with are Christians. Our social activities outside work are largely tied up with our church and with Christian friends with the result that, not deliberately, but in effect, we have drifted out of contact and out of reach of the non-Christian world. That is the first reason. The second is that some people have considered the Bible's teaching on being different and separate, and have made a deliberate decision to withdraw from the world. The aim is noble: to be holy, to become more like Jesus Christ; but I hope we will see that though being like Jesus does mean being different from the world, it does not mean withdrawing from the world. For Jesus managed somehow to be fully within reach of those who would not normally have been thought of as religious or interested in him as a religious teacher. He mixed with the tax collectors and sinners, with the prostitutes and with the social outcasts and yet there is no hint of compromise in his lifestyle or in his character.

So, whether we have drifted out of contact with the non-Christian world or whether we have made a definite decision to withdraw from the world, we need first of all to see the importance of making contact with the world. Once we have seen that our lives should be directed outwards, then we will look practically at how we can do that, trying to find different ways in which we can begin to build bridges from ourselves out into the world.

The verse that forms the focus of this chapter comes from the prayer of Jesus in John 17. Jesus says this of his disciples: 'As you sent me into the world, so I have sent them into the world' (John 17.18). There are two very strong themes running through this verse and through the passage from which it comes. One is the theme of similarity: Just as you, Father, sent me, so I too, in a similar way, am sending them. The second theme is the idea of succession. Jesus is saying 'You, Father, sent me and I am sending them in succession to me, to carry on what I have begun.' For Jesus not only prays for the disciples but also for those who will believe as a result of their words. He sees the succession going on and on. So the baton of his word, if you like, will be passed on as in a relay race from generation to generation. Jesus is to be seen first of all as our model; but also we are to see ourselves as continuing the work that he began, we are his successors as we go into the world.

The parallel is obviously not complete between Jesus' mission and our mission. This prayer was prayed the night before Jesus died. When he went to the cross that was the climax of his mission, to die in our place and to take away the penalty of our sin and rebellion against God. We cannot in any way imitate that death which he died nor its consequences. But even though the parallel is not complete it is very striking nonetheless. Jesus portrays the mission of his disciples, and by implication our mission as well, in similar terms to his own. I want to look at three areas of similarity between Jesus' mission and ours.

The Same Place

The first is that we are sent to the same place. Jesus said 'As you sent me into the world, so I have sent them into the world'. We, like Jesus, are sent into the world. The idea of being sent was very important to Jesus. Five times at least in this chapter he describes himself as the one whom God the Father had sent. He wanted people to come to believe that he was the one whom the Father had sent. As this idea of being sent into the world was important to Jesus, so it is important also to us to see ourselves as those sent into the world. We only have to look at the Church and at the lives of most of us as Christians to see that we are not fulfilling this commission very well. By and large we are not good at going into the world. In the world's view the Church and most Christians are out of touch with the world. Many of us are collected in little holy huddles around the country, in little, comfortable, cosy groups of Christians. We may occasionally have brief contact with the world but in the sense Jesus means it here we are not going out into the world.

That accusation could never have been made of Jesus; and he, as we have already shown, is our model. The purpose of a model, of course, is to give an example to follow. I am learning to play golf at the moment, caught up in the current success of European golf. I have discovered, however, that it is not as easy as it looks. A few lessons have therefore been essential. The most helpful thing about these lessons has been when my teacher has taken the golf club and given me a demonstration of how it should be done. Using his action as a model is beginning to make a difference – slowly! When it comes to thinking about our mission, Jesus is the supreme model. Watching him in action is one of the best ways to learn. So how did he fulfil this commission from his Father to go into the world? There are many examples of it; but one of the most striking instances of Jesus fulfilling this commission is seen in the company that he kept, by the fact that Jesus chose to spend time with tax collectors and sinners. The gospel writers tell many stories of his mingling with those who were normally considered to be social outcasts. His opponents objected to this strongly. We are told on other occasions that amongst his followers were those who were prostitutes and he welcomed them. We read of him touching lepers whom nobody else would touch. Jesus did not keep himself to himself. He didn't play safe in his relationships. He didn't stick with the like-minded or the religious. He went out to everybody, out into the world. He said to Zaccheus the tax collector, 'The Son of Man came to seek and to save that which is lost.' That was his understanding of his own role, to be going out, as the Father had sent him, into the world. And he is our model. We like him are sent into the world. That is where we belong as Christians.

Our calling as Christians is not to form little cliques or

holy huddles. Our calling as Christians is not to be an inward-looking group but to be an outward-looking group. Exactly how we can go about this we will think about in the next chapter. For the moment, I want us to grasp the direction we are meant to be going in. The whole direction of our lives is meant to be into the world.

The Same Character

There is, however, a second area of similarity between our mission and the mission of Jesus. It is that as we go we are meant to bear the same character that he bore. Good leaders always make their mark on the people they lead. Something of their own character and style is always imprinted on those they lead. Think of it in terms of football teams. Take two very different managers like Brian Clough and Kenny Dalgleish – one quite outspoken, the other very softly spoken. Both are very effective but their teams reflect a different style taken from the character of their leaders. Maybe you're not into football. Perhaps you like music. The same could be said of an orchestra. You can have the same orchestra playing the same piece of music, but with a different conductor, and the whole style and feel will be different, because different leaders bring out their own style and character in the ones they lead. In our mission to the world Jesus is our model not only in terms of showing us the direction our lives should follow – into the world – but also in showing us the style that should characterise our lives as we go.

What is that character? Earlier in John 17 Jesus says of his disciples, 'They are not of the world even as I am not of the world' (John 17.14). It is drawn out in his prayer in the following verses: 'My prayer is not that you take them out of the world but you protect them from the evil one.' Jesus knew that in sending his disciples into the world he was sending them on a dangerous mission. In one of his letters John states that the whole world is in the grip of the evil one. Yet he also prays specifically that they should not be taken out of the world. That is the easy way to be protected from the evil one. His message is that he wants them in the world but he doesn't want them to become of the world. The place he wants us in is the same place he was in – the world. The character he wants us to bear is not the world's character but his.

It has almost become a cliché in Christian circles to speak of being 'in the world but not of the world'. That is sad because it is such an important balance for us to grasp and to seek to achieve in our lives. What was so striking about Jesus' ministry was that he was right in the midst of the world, mingling with all sorts and types of people, and yet clearly distinct from them. That is what we are to be like as well. The balance is very difficult to achieve and most of us vere one way or the other.

Some of us are thoroughly in the world. We've got many non-Christian friends with whom we spend a great deal of time but our trouble is that there is no difference between us and our non-Christian friends. We talk their language, for instance. There is no difference between the way we speak and the way they speak. The words we use, the whole tone of our language is the same. We have picked up the negative, critical, cynical language of our day and our conversations and language reflect that. Or we go out to the pub and have a few drinks and it's as likely that we will have a few too many as that they will. Others among us are very different from the world. We don't drink, we don't smoke, a rude word never passes our lips. We withdraw from the world.

In the first case our lives most certainly touch the lives of non-Christians. There is no problem about making contact; but there is no power to our touch because there is no difference in our lives. In the second case there is no contact at all. We are out of touch, out of reach, out of contact with the world. Jesus makes it clear in his prayer that the direction of our lives should be out into the world, the same direction as his life so that we can make real contact with the world; but he also makes it clear that the character we are to bear is to be the same character that he bore so that the contact we make is an effective and powerful contact. It is a tall order and I am well aware of that, not just in theory but from my own experience; but there is good news in the third area of similarity between our mission and the mission of Jesus.

The Same Support

As we go out into the world we can know the same support that Jesus knew. In the last chapters of John's Gospel, from which our verse comes, there is a strong idea of similarity between the relationship which Jesus shared with his Father and that which we can share with Jesus. Just as he and the Father were one, so we and he are one. The idea of depending on the support of another is common. Jesus depended again and again on the support of his Father. That's why he prayed the night before he died, the night before that critical day of his life. Jesus prayed because he knew he was dependent upon his Father for support; and Jesus taught his disciples to depend upon the support that he in turn would give to them. In many ways the hardest thing about going out on a difficult assignment is the feeling of being unsupported and isolated. I don't know if you have had that experience. Perhaps there has been a job that nobody else wants to do, a customer to go and see that no-one else wants to go and see because they are difficult. You happen to be the junior in the office and so you get sent out to do the dirty work. No-one else wants anything to do with it, so you get hoisted out on your own and you find yourself making the contact, feeling unsupported and totally isolated. A very unpleasant feeling. Now that is not true of the mission Jesus sends us out on.

As Jesus sends us out he sends us fully supported and never isolated. There are many different types of support which he gives us. There is the support of his word, that baton that we thought of earlier as being passed on from generation to generation. On the one hand it is God's power for salvation as we already thought but on the other hand it can support us in our mission, so that even as we go the baton that we carry with us has its own power. Then again there is the support of his word in that it acts as our guide. So Jesus says 'Sanctify them (that is, make them different) by the truth; your word is truth'. As we seek to be in the world but not of the world God's word is our support and our guide.

Furthermore we will have the support of his cross. He goes on to say 'For them I sanctify myself, that they may be truly sanctified'. It seems to be an allusion to his death on the cross which took place the day after. Jesus knew that he was setting himself apart, sanctifying himself, to go to the cross, to die there for the sins of the whole world, to make forgiveness possible, meaning that we can always make a new start in the Christian life. In most relay races it is not possible to start again. In a 4 by 100 metres relay if you drop the baton, that's it. You've had it. By the time you pick it up again all the other teams will have finished. The race is over. But in the race of which we are thinking we may well be aware that we've dropped the baton; we may well be aware of having failed in our responsibiity to pass on God's word to others. But there's always the possibility of a second chance – and a third and a fourth and so on. For every time we are aware of failure we have the support of Jesus Christ, the forgiveness that he made possible, the acceptance and love that is always there through him. Therefore we need never go away feeling guilty or feeling we've let him down. Instead we always have the support of his cross to which we can come and confess and then start again.

Finally there is the support of his prayer for us. He was there in the garden praying for his disciples; but then he says 'My prayer is not for them alone. I pray also for those who will believe in me through their message' (John 17.20). Jesus was not only praying for his disciples, he was praying for us. The letter to the Hebrews tells us that 'he ever lives to intercede for us'. He is there today, at the right hand of the Father, praying for us. So when we go out into the world, we may have forgotten to pray, but he hasn't. He is there at the Father's right hand, interceding for us. Perhaps this is the most important support of all, the support of our relationship with him, that wherever we go we are never on our own. Many of us love that promise at the end of Matthew's gospel: 'Lo, I am with you always, to the close of the age.' It is good to remember that that promise is given following the command to go into all the world and make disciples of all nations; and 'Lo (and then)' says Jesus 'I am with you always'. There is a special way in which as we go out on this mission, sent by Jesus into the world, we have the support of his presence with us.

Making contact with the world is vital if we are to touch the lives of others with the good news of Jesus Christ. Once we see that this is what we are meant to be doing we are bound to ask 'But how can I do it? How, in practice, can I actually begin to change the direction of my life? How can I get out of my holy huddle and back into the world and yet at the same time remain not of the world?' It is these questions that we will try to answer as practically as possible in the next two chapters.

5: Every Which Way You Can

'I have become all things to all men that I might by all means save some. I do it all for the sake of the gospel that I may share in its blessings' (1 Corinthians 9.22–3).

In many ways these verses demonstrate some of the things we have been thinking about so far. They show how Paul's whole life was given over to the world of the good news. He wanted to make Jesus and his good news known. He felt compelled, under a commission, to preach the gospel. 'Woe to me', he says, 'if I do not preach the gospel.' He makes sure he does everything for the sake of the gospel. David Prior writes of Paul in his commentary on 1 Corinthians: 'Every encounter, every personal habit was now overtly under the control of Jesus Christ as Lord, because the gospel dominated Paul's whole life.' So Paul expresses this desire by saying that he wants to win as many people as possible. He wants by all means, by all possible means, to save some. It is that little phrase which is going to dominate our thinking in this chapter. Our question concerns how we can fulfil the commission that God gives us through Jesus Christ to go into the world and to take the good news with us as we go.

First, in order to give us a framework for our practical thinking together I want to look at two principles from these verses which shaped Paul's lifestyle as he tried to reach out to the world with the good news of Jesus Christ. When we have looked at those two principles we will apply them to two particular areas. First to our own lives as individuals and then to our own churches and the way we conduct ourselves there.

People must be Won

The first principle I notice here for Paul is his understanding that people must be won. That word 'win' comes five times in four verses. Literally it means to gain or to make profit. It is a business word. It speaks of the need to go and find people on the one hand and then when we have found them to win or to persuade them in the face of competition or opposition from others on the outside. There are many Christians who don't like taking business or commercial ideas or practice and applying them either to the way we run our churches or the way we get involved in the work of the good news. To be sure, there are many things that go on in the business world today which we would not want to imitate in seeking to take the good news to the world. There are, however, a number of things from which we can learn.

The principle of the need to win customers is a key principle that we could well take on board. That is, first of all, to get their attention and let them know that we are there and what we are doing, and then to win them from the competition. My wife runs her own maternity wear business. She knows very well that her first task is to let people know that she is there. Then she has to win them by showing them that she is providing something other people aren't providing and to persuade them to become her customers rather than anyone else's. And that's just our job. There are many people who have no idea what Jesus Christ offers. Many of them don't know that what Jesus offers is so much better than all the other things that are being pushed at them, day by day, through the media and through all sorts of other channels, the different philosophies, the 'isms' and 'ologies' of today's materialistic and pluralistic society. They don't know that what Jesus offers is far, far superior and they need to be won.

Many people today in the Church have the attitude that our task is to sit and wait for people to come to us. Then when they come to us and they express an interest we tell them the good news. But no businessman does that. No businessman with a product to sell says 'I'll set up my office here. I'll have everything out on my desk and then I'll wait for people to come and ask to buy my products.' No, they go out seeking to win customers. Similarly, Paul knew that people needed to be won for Jesus Christ. That is the first principle that we need to grasp.

We must be Flexible

The second principle that comes from these verses follows on from the first. It is that if people need to be won then we must be flexible. There is another saying in the business world that the customer is always right. It may be that you work now or have worked in the retail trade. If so, you have doubtless been told that when a customer comes in, whatever they want, even if it is not what you think is right, they are right. If the customer is buying a suit and wants to have his trousers half way down his calves rather than the normal length then the customer is right, and you shorten them to that length. The customer is always right. In the work of the good news we need to develop something of this kind of attitude, that in many circumstances, the outsider or the unbeliever is always right, that the outsider or the unbeliever matters most.

Certainly Paul grasped this principle. He himself had become as flexible as he possibly could be. He was willing in many different circumstances to put himself out to remove every obstacle to the progress of the good news. So, for instance, when it came to the matter of financial support that he mentions earlier in the passage: he was entitled as an apostle, as a preacher of the good news, to receive financial support from the Corinthian church but he waived that right because he didn't want to put any obstacles in the way of the good news. He was flexible and put himself out considerably, working very hard at his tent-making to make sure that he could support himself financially. He was flexible too in his behaviour. When he was with Jews he behaved like a Jew. When he was with those who weren't Jews he behaved like someone who was not a Jew. In every circumstance he was flexible, he adapted himself. To quote David Prior's commentary again, 'He became a veritable social chameleon, able to be flexible enough to change the colours of his behaviour and character according to the circumstances in which he was.' Yet within that there is no hint of compromise on the essential issues either of moral behaviour or of the truth. In the second letter to the Corinthians Paul says that he has renounced disgraceful and underhanded ways, he refuses to practise cunning or to tamper with God's word. He won't compromise the truth or his own moral standards; but in things that are secondary, things that don't really matter, he was as flexible as he possibly could be.

I want to take those two principles – that people must be won and that we must be flexible – and apply them now first to our own lives and then to our church lives.

Our Own Lives

I wonder what our own attitude is to the principle that people must be won. It's easy to sound very spiritual when justifying an attitude which encourages us to sit back and wait for people to come to us. So we might say, for instance, 'I'm waiting for the Lord to bring me someone. I pray to the Lord and I am waiting for him to lead me into evangelism.' The principle God gives us in the Bible is that people need to be won and therefore we need to go. Do we see ourselves as Paul saw himself as a slave of all? Being a slave means putting ourselves out. How are we to apply this in practice?

It applies partly to the company we keep, which we began to think about in the last chapter. We thought about the company that Jesus kept and how he took risks and didn't necessarily stick with the like-minded. For us, as committed Christians, it is so much easier to stick in the cosy Christian clique. It is much easier if we are surrounded by people who are supportive, who agree with us and with whom we agree. It makes life so much more straightforward. There is nothing wrong with supportive Christian friendship; but the best friendships are those which support us as we go out. That is the purpose of fellowship. Fellowship in New Testament terms is fellowship in the work of the gospel. All too often we want to enjoy the fellowship of Christian friends but we don't want to get involved in the work of the good news. Alternatively we bemoan the lack of fellowship and complain about the in-fighting in our church. What we fail to see is that true fellowship stems out of a concern for the good news and is fed by a concern for the good news. Take away that element and fellowship loses its meaning. It is interesting to see that Paul describes his relationship with the Philippians, to whom he seems to have been particularly close, as a 'partnership in the gospel'. That should be true of all of our Christian friendships as we encourage one another in the work of the good news.

However when it comes to relationships with non-Christians, you may say that at the moment you honestly don't know many, or even any, people who are not yet believers. So how can we begin to make those contacts that we were thinking about in the last chapter? How can I put myself out so that I can start to change the company I keep? In the first place we need to make more of our existing contacts. Most of us do have a great many non-Christian contacts unless we are hermits or live in a monastery. We have contacts at work or at school or college; we have contacts with our neighbours at home; we probably meet some people regularly at the shops or at the school gates or in other public places. There are possibilities of building on all sorts of existing relationships.

It may be that we hardly know people and so we have to start with the staple diet of all British conversation, the weather. We could move on from there to travelling or work. 'How long have you been working here? Do you enjoy it? It is pretty boring I should think at certain times of day.' A little bit about your work, forming a relationship stage by stage; but it can build up. There might be something about their families; you discover they are going through exams or whatever. 'How did they go?' Stage by stage and over a period of time a relationship can be built up. It may take some time before we see any fruit from that relationship. We may never see anything coming from it, but we will have made some contact. We will have begun to touch the lives of those people in a more meaningful way than the way we are at the moment and, who knows, something of Jesus Christ may be communicated.

Though we could all make more of our existing contacts most of us will also need to use our imagination for making new ones. Very often as Christians when we do seek to make contact with the outside world, we do it in rather unnatural ways. We go for the most difficult ways of making contact, going out and knocking on the doors of strangers or approaching passers-by in the street, for instance. Now I admire people who do that and I know that people have come to Christ that way. I don't want to knock that (forgive the pun!)—we must rejoice with the angels over all who come to Christ. What I do want to say, being realistic and honest, is that most of us could no more do those things than fly. Many of us think that that is what it means to go out into the world; and because we would never dream of doing that or something similar, we never begin to get involved in reaching out to others for Christ. However there are much easier and more natural ways of making new contacts in the world.

What about thinking about our own interests, following through some hobby or interest we have and pursuing it in a group with others? Why not join a sports club or choir (other than the church choir!)? Or, if you are going on holiday somewhere abroad, why not go to an evening class to learn a particular language? Or it may be you have got some obscure interest in medieval Chinese art or something which you have been meaning to follow up for a long time. You discover that your local council is running an evening class on it. When you turn up at the class and meet others, you may have nothing else in common but medieval Chinese art. This may be rather an obscure thing to have in common but it is a bridge on which something else can be built. It could be that you've been meaning to start frequenting your local, to try to get into the darts team. We need to think of different ways in which we can meet with those who are not yet Christians on a level, in an ordinary and natural way. I have taken up golf, partly because I need the exercise, but also because it is a sociable game and a way therefore of meeting people. It's difficult for those of us cooped up in churches all day to meet people outside.

One of the most refreshing experiences I have had over the last year was being invited to lead a Christian skiing holiday. Though it was good to be with the group of Christians, it was particularly good to be an ordinary member of a ski class. It was my first time skiing as it was for everybody in our class. That was all that we had in common. We were from different parts of the country, different social backgrounds; but on the ski slopes we were together on equal terms. I wish that I could say that by the end of the week they were all converted; but that did not happen. However there were one or two opportunities to say something and who knows what effect they had. The important thing for me was that it was real and natural contact. I find the same thing with the involvement that I have in my wife's business. It gives me a number of outside contacts and it is very refreshing from that point of view.

What about our neigbours? I was hearing recently from some friends who were staying with us that they were thinking of ways they could invite their neighbours to their home using Christmas as a natural opportunity. Christmas is a great time for that sort of thing. Everyone suddenly feels a bit religious at Christmas. They decided to have open house one evening with mince-pies, mulled wine and

Christmas carols. They have a very musical curate at their church and they were planning to get him to come along and busk away on the piano and sing a few carols – not to give a talk, just to natter about the carols in between each one. We need to use our imagination thinking of many different ways, individually and in small groups, to reach out and make new contacts.

Our Church Life

Let us now apply these principles – that people must be won, and that we therefore must be flexible – to the life of our own churches. It was William Temple, Archbishop of Canterbury, who said 'The Church is the only institution in the world which exists primarily for the benefit of non-members.' But of how many churches could that be truthfully said? We may be working towards it. I hope we are working towards it in *our* church, but I'm not sure I could put my hand on my heart and say it is absolutely true of us. We have it in mind. We are heading in that direction; but we have a long way to go.

So much of our church life is self-indulgent and highly inflexible: we run our churches according to very strict patterns and very much for the benefit of the insider not the outsider. We need to look at the way we behave on Sundays when we meet together. How do we decide on our attitude towards what happens in our church on a Sunday? What questions do we ask? Isn't the question we normally ask, do we like it? Did I like that service? Did I like that song? Did it do anything for me? Or if we are in positions of leadership in a church the question we might well ask is 'What can we get away with by way of a balance between all the various sections in the church to keep most of the people happy most of the time?' Aren't those two things the things that dictate most of what happens in our churches on a Sunday? How often do we ask the much more important question, 'How would an unbeliever or an outsider feel if they came into our church? What would they make of what we are doing here? How would they get on? Would they feel at home and welcome or would they feel totally excluded? Would they come in and think we were mad (as in Paul's example in 1 Corinthians 14)?'

We need to work towards a pattern that creates the sort of atmosphere into which the enquiring outsider or unbeliever can come and feel at home and not threatened, free to feel round the edges without immediately being button-holed. Many of those who are hurting because they have gone through difficult things in life come to the church because they feel somehow we may be able to help. It is vital that they can come in and find an atmosphere which is welcoming, that they can find something going on with which they can identify and some of which they can understand, so that they can begin to be helped.

We need to look at our language, not only in the services we hold but in the way we talk to and about one another. We need to examine that awful Christian jargon which we use, which must be largely incomprehensible to the outsider. I was watching a baseball game on television the other evening. Now I reckon with American football I understand one word in two, sometimes better, but with the baseball game I was flummoxed. I hadn't a clue what was going on. It seemed to me that they were playing with a ball; but that they could throw a ball and it wasn't a ball. And sometimes it was a strike and sometimes it was a ball and sometimes it didn't seem to be anything at all. I could not work this jargon out. So I was bored silly. It might have been a fascinating game. I suspect it was very close, very interesting. But I was excluded because I didn't understand the jargon. I suspect that many outsiders who come in to our churches or who hear Christians talk haven't a clue what we are going on about. Why, for instance, do we have to say 'We are going to have a short time of worship'? This means nothing to the outsider. If we tell him we are going to sing a few songs, he knows what we are going to do. Why do we say that someone is going to come up and give their testimony? What on earth is a testimony – isn't it what happens in court in American TV programmes? Why can't we tell people that someone is going to come and tell us about what Jesus Christ means to them in their own lives, about how they came to know him for themselves? Then they might have some idea of what is going to happen next. Or consider even the way we talk about 'the Lord'. I know we need to submit to Jesus as Lord and in many ways our desire to refer to Jesus as 'the Lord' is the right desire; but it can sound incredibly pious to the outsider. Why can't we talk about Jesus and about God; or, if we want to use the phrase 'the Lord', talk about the Lord Jesus Christ so that they know who we are talking about? I think we need to look carefully at our use of language.

There was an article recently in the *Guardian* newspaper describing how someone who was not a committed Christian visited three churches one Sunday (he was a glutton for punishment!). One of the things that put him off in one church was that the two people who came up to lead the prayers were introduced by their Christian names alone, as John and Jane or whatever their names were. The writer's point was that the insider knew who they were but he, as the outsider, hadn't a clue. This doesn't mean that we should stop using each other's Christian names, but perhaps a little more explanation for the benefit of the outsider might be helpful. You may say that it doesn't matter in your church because there are never any outsiders there! Well if the Christians in the church sort themselves out there soon will be; and it's best to get ready for them now!

The last area I want us to think about is perhaps one of the most important and will call for major surgery in the lives of many of our churches. It concerns the way we use people within our churches and the way we organise our church programme. Is our church life so full of activity, for instance, of one sort or another that frankly there is no time for getting out and making new contacts? If we are busy four or five evenings a week with Christian activities, how can we possibly have time to get involved in some outside activity where we might make new contacts with people who don't yet know Christ? And what is our reaction to someone new and gifted as a Christian who arrives at our church? Do we immediately think of all the ways they could be used within the life of the church? Let me paint an all too familiar picture.

It's great that Sue has come along to our church. She is really gifted. You know we've got that need in the Sunday School class. We must get her in there. Then there's the midweek fellowship group. I gather that she has done some Bible school training. We must get her leading one of those Bible studies. She is pretty musical, too, so we have got to have her singing in the choir. Soon poor Sue is up to her ears in Christian activity because of the way we run our churches. Is it too much to hope that we could change the way we think in this area? Let me paint a more hopeful picture.

Sue is a very gifted girl, she makes friends easily. We must make sure she has got time to be out meeting people and making contacts. What's the most strategic use we can make of her in the church while at the same time leaving her free to develop relationships outside as well? At our church we have agreed that whenever possible no one should spend more than three evenings a week in regular church activities: Sundays at church, Tuesdays either at our Prayer Gathering or in one of our fellowship groups, and one other evening for training or for the choir or in youth work or whatever. For many people that will not involve much change, but for those at the heart of the church it will mean big changes if ever we manage to put it into operation! For, in my experience, whether a church is large or small there is nearly always a group of people who are tied up with church activities four, five or even six evenings a week. How can we possibly expect them then to be able to go out into the world and make contact with those who don't yet know Christ? There's only so much time in a day. Perhaps we need to do some hard thinking and some rationalising of our own activities if we are going to be effective in reaching out with the good news of Christ. It may be too that those of us in full-time church work need to be the first to examine our lifestyles.

To conclude, we need to ask these hard questions of ourselves. We need to apply these principles that people must be won and that we must be flexible. We must apply them to our own lives as individuals and also to our own church life even if it means doing some fairly drastic reorganisation of our own lives or of our own churches. But until we do that we will never make effective contact with the world that needs to hear the good news of Jesus Christ.

6: The Natural Life

We have been thinking in the last two chapters about the
need to make contact with the world in which we live, and
with those who don't yet know Jesus Christ personally. The
last chapter was about the need to make contact in every
possible way that we can imagine: to make the most of the
opportunities we already have, but also to try to find new
ways to make real and meaningful contact with other
people. Yet in nearly every instance, the first way in which
we make contact with people is by the touch, not of what we
say, but of what we are; the touch of our lives. Rarely do we
begin a relationship with a conversation about the good
news. Normal relationships begin when two lives touch.
Often the first stage is one of observation. We look at their
lives; they look at ours. All sorts of factors influence our
reaction, what they look like, how they behave, the way
they speak. A form of social fencing takes place as we decide
if this is going to be a relationship we want to cultivate or
terminate! The longer this process goes on the less the
superficial things like looks and accents matter. Instead the
main yardstick becomes what we make of them as people.
Are their lives attractive? Are we drawn towards them?
What we need to remember is that just as we are coming to
conclusions about them as people, so too they are assessing
us.

Paul was obviously aware of this when he said to the
Philippians 'only let your manner of life be worthy of the
gospel of Christ' (Philippians 1.27). That sentence is going

to be the main focus of our thinking in this chapter. The word Paul uses here for 'worthy' is an interesting word. It means literally 'of equal value'. It is a word taken from the market place. So, for instance, if you buy a particular item from a shop and get it home only to discover that it doesn't work, you take it back and ask them to change it. Now they might say that they have got none of that particular model left at the moment. They would then offer you something else that corresponds to what you originally purchased. That is the meaning of the word 'worthy'. Paul knew that it was very important that our lives and our behaviour should correspond to the good news we are seeking to pass on, so that when someone who is not yet a Christian hears the message we speak and looks at the lives that we lead they will say 'Yes, the two tie up, they are telling the same story.' Our lives should be the most powerful visual aid we can possibly have for the good news itself.

Interestingly, Paul makes clear earlier in the same passage that the good news is so powerful that even when it is preached from wrong motives it can still be effective; but in what he says to the Philippians we can see that his ideal is that the speaking of the good news and the life of the speaker should be comparable. From the context it is clear that he is talking about their manner of life both as individuals and as a group of Christians together. I don't know if you ever have to represent the company or firm you work for. If you do, you will be representing your firm or company as an individual; but in the way you represent the company and in the whole service that follows on from your original contact, the person concerned will come into contact not only with you as an individual but with the company as a whole. The good name of the company depends both on our behaviour as individuals and also on the whole way in which the company works together, the back-up, the support, the efficiency and so on. So too the Christian good news needs to be backed up both by our lives as individual Christians and also by the life of the church. Our manner of life, corporately and individually, needs to be worthy of the good news. But what does Paul mean by this in practice? A number of things might spring into our minds of what is worthy of the good news but it is interesting to see what Paul actually chooses to draw out in this passage.

United in the Gospel

The first mark of a life worthy of the gospel that Paul mentions is a corporate mark, that we should be united in the gospel. Having said that our manner of life must be worthy of the gospel of Christ he goes on to say in the same verse 'so that whether I come and see you or am absent, I may hear of you that you stand firm in one Spirit with one mind striving side by side for the faith of the gospel'. But why is this unity in the gospel so important for a life that is worthy of the gospel? Surely it is because the message of the good news is a unifying message. It is a message that proclaims the love of God, a message that breaks down, says Paul, the barriers between God and man, and also the barriers between one man and another. Paul tells the Galatian Christians that there is therefore in Christ neither Jew nor Greek, neither slave nor free, neither male nor female but all are one in Christ Jesus.

The gospel message has within it the whole idea of unity; for the gospel unites men with God, and men and women with one another. But if someone who is not yet a Christian hears this good news, this message which should lead to unity, and yet looks at Christians and sees that we are divided and are constantly squabbling with one another, that there is no love lost between us, then that person will say that the two things do not correspond. The life and the message do not tie up together. But if the same person hears the same message and looks at a group of Christians and sees that despite their differences in age, race, background and interest, there is an extraordinary unity, they will say 'Yes, these two things do correspond. Their lives and their message tell the same story.'

We have probably all been taken in by advertisements which proclaim one thing but in practice never seem to live up to what is proclaimed. I was watching a soap powder ad the other evening, a new form of a famous brand which now washes even whiter than it ever did before. They proclaimed before that it could get any stain out; the new claim is that any stain that it *couldn't* previously get out, it now *can* remove. Now I don't know whether the stains that our family manage to put on clothes are much tougher than the stains the advertisers use; but for us they never quite seem to live up to the claims that are made. It is so important, you see, that what we are and what we say correspond if the good news is to be heard and accepted; and it is particularly important that a message which proclaims there need be no barriers between God and man and between man and man should be reflected in our unity as groups of Christians. But how is this unity achieved?

The answer lies in the very message of the good news itself. For if, as we were thinking in the first chapter, we understand the good news then we will understand that all of us are Christians on one basis only, through the central message of the gospel of Jesus and him crucified. We will understand that the Christian good news is a message which levels us out; though we may be different in the world's eyes in many ways, in the eyes of the good news and in God's eyes we are on a level, for all of us need to come to the cross of Jesus Christ to find forgiveness and peace with God. Every relationship with him begins at the cross. Therefore any ideas of superiority or inferiority within a group of Christians who understand the message of the good news is totally out of place.

Furthermore, if we understand the good news we will want to share it and that will be a number one priority in our lives. Now this shared desire together with the knowledge that we are all on a level in the light of the message of the good news are two of the most powerful unifying forces that exist in the Christian life. Where Christian groups have recognised that these things exist, that we are on a level in the light of the good news and that we are committed to sharing that good news with others, then great unity has been achieved and great things have been done for God. The Christian Union movement in the universities and colleges of our land and overseas is a fine example of how these two principles can be very effective unifying factors. There have been differences within the movement over baptism, over spiritual gifts and their use, over styles of worship, all sorts of differences which people have exercised in other ways, but members have committed themselves together to the work of the good news without passing judgement on one another in these other matters. The result has been that thousands of students have been won for Jesus Christ through their work.

I think, too, of mission teams that I have been privileged to serve on. It's extraordinary how when you gather together with a common desire to share the gospel, all sorts of differences seem so much less important. This can happen in ordinary churches as well, for the good news itself is the source of Christian unity and when that Christian unity exists it is a very powerful visual aid to the truth of the message. We need therefore to reassess our own priorities, we need to decide what is secondary and concentrate on what is primary so that we can know unity in the work of the good news. We need to learn to put aside our own particular likes and dislikes for the benefit of the work of the good news; for the first mark of a life that is worthy of the gospel is that together we should be united in the gospel.

Suffering for the Gospel

The second mark is that our lives will be characterised by suffering for the gospel. Again, that is not necessarily what we would immediately expect. It is, however, what Paul moves on to next, for to him it was a fundamental aspect of Christian living, especially for those who get involved in the work of the good news. He speaks in the following verse of the possibility of his readers' being frightened by their opponents. It's quite clear to Paul that if they decide to stand side by side for the gospel there will be opposition. He goes on to tell them that it has been granted to them (they must have been pleased about this) that for the sake of Christ they should not only believe in him but also suffer for his sake. Interesting phraseology, isn't it? Paul says it has been 'granted to you', it is a privilege, not only to believe in Jesus Christ but also to suffer for his sake particularly in the context of the work of the good news. But why should the business of passing on the good news involve suffering or difficulty? Why? – because once again it corresponds with the message.

If our lives are to reflect our message, they are bound to involve suffering for the gospel, for our message is a message about a suffering Saviour. It is about Jesus Christ and him crucified, nailed to a cross. Throughout the New Testament Jesus, Paul and the other apostles make it quite clear that being a Christian will involve following Jesus in terms of his cross, so that the message we preach and the lives we lead are bound to correspond. It won't necessarily mean a physical cross or even physical suffering. It is unlikely to mean that for us here in the West; but it does mean that if we choose to stand up for the gospel as individuals and together as a body, we will not always enjoy undiluted popularity. The most common forms of suffering that we face here in the West are ridicule and personal rejection. These may sound tame when compared to the physical suffering of many of our brethren in other parts of the world; yet they are still very real forms of suffering, if we decide to stand up for Jesus Christ and him crucified.

A Christian husband and wife found that there was a period when, every time they came into a room, those they worked with would start raising their hands in the air and saying 'Praise the Lord'. They found it very difficult to take. They were being ridiculed and it was very uncomfortable. On another occasion the woman was talking with a friend about what they had both been like as teenagers. He was confessing to some of the things that he got up to as a teenager, and he looked at her and said 'I suppose the worst thing you got up to was being told off for praying too much.' Neither of these things is particularly serious when compared to more severe forms of suffering. However if they come repeatedly when we are under pressure, and if they come from those we love and whom we are seeking to bring to Christ, then they can be very hurtful indeed. We need to recognise that things like that will happen to us, that we will be on the receiving end of that form of opposition if we choose to make a stand for Jesus Christ. It may seem very childish but we all know that it can be very hurtful. It can be a very real form of suffering for the gospel and it is bound to happen, says Paul, it is part of a life which is worthy of the gospel. We need to be prepared for it.

There is much talk today that if we are speaking a message about the kingdom of God then our lives should display the power of the kingdom of God; but the New Testament emphasis is very different. The New Testament emphasis is that if we are speaking a message about Jesus Christ and him crucified then our lives should correspond and we should be prepared to suffer for the gospel. The triumph of the kingdom will be seen; but the New Testament pattern is that it is not seen in our lives for our experience will be that of suffering for the gospel. The triumph will be seen in the lives of others as their lives are transformed, as they turn to God and receive new life through God's Holy Spirit. There is a crying need in the Church today to rediscover the message of the cross not only in what we preach but also in our expectation of what it will be like to preach it.

One of the major factors that causes Christians to drop out of the Christian life is that we find it much harder being a Christian than we thought it would be. Much of this comes from our teaching a shallow gospel that makes few demands on us and which does not present Jesus as Lord. However if there are many who give up the Christian life altogether when they find the going gets tough, there are also many who give up the work of the good news because it's too difficult. If at any stage I have given the impression that I think that this work is easy then let me correct it now. Being involved in the work of the good news means suffering for the good news. It always will do. There will be people we grow to love dearly but who turn their backs on the gospel and maybe on us as well. There will be ridicule. There may be opposition from Christian friends who don't share our vision. No one can predict what form it will take at any given time; but we can be sure of this one thing, that suffering for the gospel is a sure mark of a life that is worthy of the gospel.

However, it is most certainly not all gloom and doom. There is more joy and fulfilment associated with reaching others for Christ than with any form of Christian service that I know of. There is, as we have already thought, a depth of fellowship which we experience when we are committed to this work which is far greater than much which passes for fellowship in many churches; but if you take on this work, you will need that fellowship and support, because it won't be easy.

Like Christ who is the Gospel

The third and final mark I want us to look at in a life worthy of the gospel is that we should be like Christ who is the gospel. That is the over-riding principle that runs throughout this passage. In one sense it contains what we have thought about in terms of being united in the gospel, for we are united in Christ; and being prepared to suffer for the gospel, which is suffering like Christ; but it is much more than that as well. Paul says that for him 'to live is Christ'. He goes on in chapter 2 to tell the Philippians how they should live. He tells them about the example of Christ and says that they should have the same mind that Jesus had in their relationship with one another. It is important to grasp this principle, that a life worthy of the gospel of Christ is a life that is like Christ who is the gospel.

Grasping this principle will lead us to ask the right questions in any given situation. What would Jesus do in this situation? How would he react? Would he speak or would he remain silent?

The New Testament puts being like Jesus at the top of its list of priorities for our lives. It is our destiny, Paul tells us. We have been predestined to be conformed to the likeness of God's son. He prays that Christ will be formed in us. We are meant to bear the family likeness, to be like Jesus Christ. My son is always being told that he looks like me. At the moment, aged eight, he thinks that is a compliment. What he will make of it when he is a teenager I don't know! In the same way there is to be a family likeness amongst God's people. We are to be like Jesus Christ; and one of the most important reasons for this is that being like Jesus is a very powerful visual aid for the good news. The subject of the good news is Jesus Christ and him crucified. The good news that we have to pass on is not a set of propositions, not a list of dos and don'ts, it is a message about a person, the person of Jesus Christ. Therefore if our lives are like his, people will hear our message which is about Jesus, they will look at our lives and say 'Yes, I see something of the person they are speaking of in the life that they lead'. When they see that, it is very powerful indeed. Many of us probably became Christians ourselves because we had that experience. We saw in the life of a Christian something of Jesus Christ, so that when we heard the message we said 'Yes, the two tie together. Their message and their lives correspond. It must be real.' But in what particular ways are we to be like Jesus Christ? Let me suggest just three areas in which it should show.

It will show in our attitude to people. The good news is for everybody, and Jesus showed this in the fact that nobody he spoke to was beyond the pale for him. Maybe there is someone we know whom everybody else thinks of as being beyond the pale. They are thought of as the lowest of the low. Nobody else has any time for them. Jesus would have done. To him, each individual mattered; and they matter to him today. He took time for people. He took time to listen. Being like Christ who is the gospel will show in our attitude to people.

It will show in our priorities. Jesus said 'My food is to do the will of my Father.' Most of us are surrounded by people whose desires are very different from the desire and priorities of Jesus Christ. The priorities that surround us are those of success, of wealth and of experience. If we share Jesus' priorities it is bound to show and people will begin to see that we are like Christ who is the gospel.

It will show too in our conversation, not just by the fact that we don't use certain swear-words that other people use; but more importantly, it will show in the whole flavour of our conversation, in our desire to be positive rather than negative, in our desire to stick by what we say, so that our word is reliable, that our yes is yes and our no is no.

The principle that we need to grasp is that people need to see something of Jesus not only in what we say but in who we are, in the way we behave, in the way we treat them. There are many other books on Christian living and we would do well to read some of them. In a culture that puts a high priority on experience it is all too easy for us as Christians to measure our Christian lives by the same yardstick. The New Testament, however, is much more concerned with the way we live, with our becoming more like Jesus Christ. This is important for its own sake, for it is our destiny to be like Christ; but it is also important for the work of the gospel, for a life that speaks of Jesus will draw people to Jesus who is the gospel.

Our lives as individuals and together need to correspond to the message of the good news that we are seeking to pass on. The message we share and the lives we lead need to tell the same story; but we need to be realistic as well. This side of heaven there never will be a complete triumph. None of us will ever lead lives that are fully worthy of the good news, either individually or together. It may be that we are aware of areas of failure, maybe even from today. We need to remember that the cross of Jesus is not only our model which leads us to expect to suffer for the gospel but it is also our source of forgiveness. It is always there. There is never a time when we cannot return to seek for God's forgiveness and make a new start. All of us need to do that again and again. None of us lead lives where there is a perfect tie-up between the message we preach and the lives we lead, for we won't reach perfection in this life, nor will the groups of Christians to which we belong reach complete unity in this life. Yet it is amazing how many who are not yet Christians will be attracted by what we feel is actually not a very good example of Christian living. We may feel that we are failing, and yet others will see something of Jesus Christ. We won't succeed fully, but if we are heading in the right direction then a life which begins to be 'worthy of the gospel' can be a very powerful visual aid to the message of the good news itself.

7: Head to Head

Ultimately we are not out just to contact people nor just to influence people by the way we live but to win people for Jesus Christ. A fisherman went home one evening and his wife asked him how he had got on that day. He replied, 'Well, I didn't catch many but I influenced a lot.' Influence is very important but our aim must be that people should hear the good news of God's love, and that hearing it they should respond in repentance and faith, turning from what they know to be wrong and trusting in Jesus Christ. If this is to happen people need to hear that good news. Therefore we need to speak the good news. We are asking someone who is not yet a Christian to commit themselves to Jesus Christ. To take that decision they need information.

In no other area of life do we take decisions without having at least some basic information. If we are considering an important move concerning our future, marriage, a new job, some form of training, we take time to find out what the options are, how they compare, where they lead to and so on. The person who is not yet a Christian needs information if they are going to make a move that will have such a radical effect on their future; and therefore we need to give that information. But from our point of view we also know that we need to speak the good news and not just live it, because when we speak the good news we know that it has an inbuilt power, that the good news itself is the power of God for salvation. Therefore, both for the sake of the outsider who needs information and because we know that the source of that information is itself powerful, we must speak about Jesus Christ. Important though it is, it's not enough just to live a life worthy of the gospel.

However, as soon as we begin to think about the whole area of speaking to other people about Jesus Christ, we need to acknowledge that it is an area in which most, if not all of us, feel inadequate. We can probably all think, if we've been Christians for any length of time, of opportunities that we have had to talk about our faith openly and naturally; yet we have failed to take those opportunities. Or we could think of other opportunities that we *did* take, but made a complete and utter pig's ear of them, either because we said far too much or because we said the wrong thing or because we said far too little. All of us feel inadequate in this area of talking about our faith and I include myself. It is a natural feeling and it's important for us to know that we all feel like that.

We all need to learn, therefore, about how we can be more effective 'head to head', about how we can both create and take opportunities to speak of Jesus Christ. In this chapter we are going to do that by looking at a short passge from Paul's letter to the Colossians. It is a lovely cameo passage both about Paul's own experience of passing on the good news to others and also about what he expected from the Colossians. It's all about opportunities and about our relationships with those who are not yet Christians.

> Continue steadfastly in prayer, being watchful in it with thanksgiving; and pray for us also, that God may open to us a door for the word, to declare the mystery of Christ, on account of which I am in prison, that I might make it clear as I ought to speak. Conduct yourselves wisely toward outsiders, making the most of the time. Let your speech always be gracious, seasoned with salt, so that you may know how you ought to answer everyone (Colossians 4.2–6).

69

Prayer is the Secret

I want to draw three lessons from this passage. The first is the obvious but very important lesson that prayer is the secret. It is easy for such a statement to seem trite, it's so obvious. Yet it is very striking how it comes across in this passage. For Paul not only tells the Colossians to continue steadfastly in prayer but he goes on to ask them to pray for him also. Why is it that Paul, with all his experience of passing on the good news, requests the prayers of the Colossians? Presumably it was because he felt inadequate for the task himself. Isn't that why we pray? We pray when we find things difficult and we know we need help. It's quite an encouragement here therefore that Paul needed help in the business of talking to others about Jesus Christ.

So if we feel inadequate, if we feel: 'Help! If I'm going to talk to others about Jesus I need not only to pray myself but I need others to pray for me', that's not surprising because that is just how Paul felt. Things that are difficult force us to pray. That's one of the good things about times that are hard in our Christian lives. How many students are there who never ever pray except when they go into the exam-room? They know it is going to be difficult. And if we make a deliberate effort and decision not only to contact people who don't yet know Jesus but also to speak to them about Jesus, then we will find that we are forced back onto God in prayer because of our own feelings of inadequacy in face of the task. But what did Paul pray for?

In the first place he prayed for opportunities. He asked the Colossians to pray that God would open a door for the Word. That is a lovely picture; he was constantly looking for doorways. If the door is ajar we can't help but peek in; if the door is closed then the door is closed, that's it. But an open door is always very inviting. Paul was always on the look-out for open doors into people's lives, some doorway through which his message could enter. We too need to pray and ask others to pray for us, that we will find doorways, that there will be opportunities to pass on the message of Jesus Christ. Most of us need to pray not only for the opportunities but also for the ability to see those opportunities. I sometimes sit down at the end of the day and look back on it and see that I have missed a whole lot of opportunities which, if I had really been awake and alert, I'd have noticed.

Paul also prayed for clarity. He asked them to pray not only for a door for the Word, but that he might make it clear as he ought to speak. The word translated 'make it clear' means literally 'to placard' the Truth. Paul wanted to make his message so clear that it was as if it was on an advertising bill-board. On the way I often drive to work I have to queue to turn right at one point. Sitting in the car, twiddling your thumbs, you have got to look at a certain bill-board because there is nothing else to do. You can't miss it. It's right in front of your eyes. It reads something like this: 'What a silly place to put a wall, right in front of our new car-hire show-room' (with the name of the company underneath). I can't remember the exact words, but the message has got through to me. If ever I wanted to hire a car or a van I would know where to go! The message has got through to me because it was placarded in front of me. It was crystal clear. I couldn't miss it. Paul says 'I want to make the Christian message that clear. I want to placard it so that everybody can see it and understand it.'

This clarity is something we can work at and that we can get better at through practice, and through thinking through the truths of the gospel, perhaps even through learning some outlines of the good news. But it is also something that we are always going to need to pray for, because no two people are the same. No two opportunities are the same. And making the message so that it can be understood by a particular individual is always going to be something we are going to have to pray for help with. We need to pray therefore before the opportunity arises that there will be opportunities and that we will see them, but also during those opportunities, so that we will have that ability to see how we can make the truth absolutely crystal

71

clear. How can I placard the truth I am trying to get across to this particular person? Prayer is the secret.

Urgency is the Motive

Secondly, urgency is the motive. Speaking to people, as we have already acknowledged, about our faith, is a difficult thing to do. We need therefore to be honest with ourselves that we will only do it if we see that it is urgent. I don't know about your life but in my life at the moment it is only the urgent that gets done. My motto is 'Why do today what I can easily put off until tomorrow?' For many of us, the business of speaking about Jesus Christ comes into that category. It's not that urgent, it can be put off until tomorrow. There'll be another opportunity, we think; or, that person is probably not interested anyway; they wouldn't want to come to our guest service that we are having at church on Sunday. The opportunity passes by because we don't have this sense of urgency. Therefore we need to grasp it. Paul demonstrates it for us superbly in this passage.

He is in prison for his work of the gospel. Now if you and I were in prison what would be top of our list of priorities? I can tell you what would be top of mine. One, freedom, as I would want to get out of prison. Two, given that that might not be possible, comfort, so that even if I had to be in prison I might have some friends to see and some home comforts. But what is at the top of Paul's list of priorities? For him, the most important thing is that whether he is in prison or free, whether he is well fed or hungry, whatever the position, there should be a door for the Word. That is what he asked them to pray for.

He passes on this feeling to the Colossians when he tells them to conduct themselves wisely towards outsiders (taking up the theme of our last chapter). But note the telling phrase, 'making the most of the time'. He wanted the Colossians too to have this sense of urgency. The phrase comes from the market-place. It's the phrase you would use of a trader who has only got a certain time to sell what is on his stall. Picture, for instance, a farmer who has brought his fresh produce down to the market-place in Colossae. There were no fridges in those days. He wouldn't want to cart it all back to his farm again. He had to sell it and he had got to sell it on the day. So he is standing there shouting out, 'Buy my tomatoes', because they have got to be bought; it's urgent; he's got to make the most of the time. That is the feeling of the word that Paul uses here.

We need to see the reality of our situation and the reality of the situation of those who don't yet know Jesus Christ. We are all too aware of our own feelings of fear and inadequacy and we need to face up to those and recognise them. There is no point in pretending that we are brave when we are not. But we also need to remind ourselves of the reality of people's needs. Can we not all think of people we know who are desperately in need of love and acceptance? They are constantly putting on a front, putting on an image, trying to make themselves acceptable to other people. Can you think of people like that? It's a cry for love and for acceptance. Now where can that be found? There is only one place, surely, and that is in Jesus Christ. There are other people going round burdened with guilt. It weighs them down. Who else, but Jesus Christ, can take that away?

We need to look at the reality of people's need and we also need to look at the reality of time. We do not have for ever. World events have a habit of reminding us of the frailty of life and of the society we have created. So much of the time it feels so secure but then there is a financial crisis, horrendous storms, a killer disease like AIDS or some other tragedy which brings home the reality of time. Time is not there for ever and Paul tells us that we are to make the most of the time. This sense of urgency communicates itself right through the pages of the New Testament and if we keep those pages open in front of us then we too will find that not only is prayer the secret but that urgency becomes our motive.

73

Tact is the Watchword

Finally, 'tact' is the watchword. The Bible has a marvellous balance in its teaching and that sense of urgency that comes through here is quickly balanced by the words 'let your speech always be gracious, seasoned with salt so that you may know how you ought to answer everyone.' There seem to be two balances here. One is the balance between the salesman or the market dealer and the fisherman, between the salesman who has got to sell everything today and the fisherman who knows that you can't hurry the fish. You have got to put the bait there; you've got to throw it in; but then you've got to wait for the fish to bite. There is also the balance that comes in the food analogy, the balance between speech which is insipid or tasteless and speech that is so spicy that it burns a hole in the back of your throat. I don't know how you like your food. I can't stand vegetables that taste of nothing because the salt has been left out, nor do I like those really hot meals that you can't taste because they simply burn your taste-buds off your tongue! I like food that has got real taste, but not too much. That, says Paul, is exactly how our speech should be to the outsider. It shouldn't be insipid. Many people see Christians as wet and insipid. We should never be like that. Other Christians are so over the top that they are over-powering, more like a hot, spicy curry. No, our speech is to be gracious and yet seasoned with salt. Tact is the watchword.

A friend told me a lovely story just this week of an experience he had, which is common to those of us who work in the West End of London. He was approached by one of the many people at Oxford Circus trying to interest passers-by in life assurance or savings.

'Excuse me, sir,' the salesman said, 'I'm from such-and-such a company. Can I interest you in some of the schemes we have to help you to save money?'

'To tell you the truth, I couldn't really give a button about money,' my friend replied.

The salesman was undaunted, however. Obviously he

had been taught a follow-up line for this particular thing and so he continued, 'Well, sir, you know money solves a lot of problems. It's good to have some.'

'I don't know about that,' my friend replied. 'I'm not sure that money does solve that many problems. It seems to me in the world today it creates at least as many problems as it solves. You know it really isn't the biggest thing in my life. I often think about that verse in the Christian Scripture that says that the love of money is the root of all evil. It's got a wonderful balance you know. It doesn't tell us that money is evil because it's not, but there is a warning there for us.'

'Oh!' said the salesman. And there the conversation ended.

My friend told me afterwards he wondered if he should have said more. He didn't mention God. He didn't mention Jesus Christ. Did he say too much or did he say too little? I personally think with that little story he got the balance just about right. Isn't that an example of speech which is seasoned with salt and yet gracious? The question that we often face when opportunities do arise is 'How much do I say?' Once we see the green light of opportunity we don't often see the red light which says stop. Knowing how far to go and when to stop is one of the critical things in learning to talk to people about our faith. Ultimately, of course, we want to get across the whole of the message of the good news, but not in one go. Otherwise, to carry on the food analogy, people get indigestion. We need to think of natural ways in which we can season our speech with salt so that people are left with something to think about. That way if they are interested then they will come back for more and there will be further opportunities. We need to aim to leave the door open.

When it comes to preparing for opportunities we need to think about the issues that are in people's minds, that naturally come into the sort of conversation we have with our friends at work or amongst our friends at home. We need to think then if there is a Christian viewpoint on those particular issues. John Chapman, the Australian evangelist, tells the story of how he agreed with a friend that they would look every day at the leader in the paper and try and make some Christian comment to each other on it. Why not try that as an exercise for a little while? What is there that a Christian has to contribute on the latest financial collapse, for example? What is our view of that? But we need to do this without being pious or sentimental which is seen as being insipid in the view of the outsider. It's not easy. We need to think about it hard and work at it. But that needs to be our aim, to have speech which is gracious and yet seasoned with salt.

We may feel 'What on earth is the significance of one small comment?' So, for instance, it was quite clever of my friend to bring in that verse but did it do any good? Well, of course, we don't know in that particular situation whether it did or didn't. But part of the whole thinking behind this book is that the effect in people's lives is a gradual one, a cumulative one, that very few people are touched just once, pow! and that's it. For most people the way they are touched by God is by a small touch here, a small touch there, in one way and another way, something they see in one person's life, something they hear another say. Yet bit by bit that touch begins to get through until they feel the touch of God. It's a process. For most it happens over a period of time and at each moment of touch, be it verbal or through the attractiveness of someone's life, only a small amount is communicated. But when God is at work opportunities will arise in time when more and more can be communicated, not just the odd comment but eventually the good news itself. It may be a direct opportunity when we talk to them ourselves or it may take the form of an opportunity to invite them to a guest service or to a discussion evening in someone's home. We may then have opportunity to follow that up afterwards more personally.

However when we do see the touch of God working in people's lives, not just to make them interested but so that they respond by turning and by trusting in Jesus Christ, we see one of the most exciting things in the whole of the

Christian life. This is especially true when friends whom we know and love come to know and love the Lord Jesus Christ for themselves. I remember vividly a friend who became a Christian after what seemed like months of discussion and being dragged along to various Christian meetings. I had often been tempted to lose heart. There were times when I thought he was merely being polite when he accepted invitations to church. Finally, however, we had a crucial conversation and he said he wanted to become a Christian. He wanted to do it on his own, so I left him to pray; but I told him to tell me as soon as he had so that we could help him on. I saw him the next day. I was dying to ask him if he'd made the step but I didn't want to force the issue. I didn't have to wait long, however, for he looked at me and said, 'Kim, I've done it!' He was beaming from ear to ear. So was I! There is little to compare with seeing the touch of God as our lives touch the lives of others. That's how most of us come to Jesus Christ. It's the natural touch.

8: Questions Need Answers

The second part of this book is, as I mentioned in the introduction, concerned with effective communication. Much of the material in it comes from my experience in helping to run a group that meets in our church. It used to be called 'Agnostics Anonymous', but is now called 'Open to Question'. It is an open group to which anyone can come. Its aim is to provide a forum in which people can air the questions that they have about life and about the Christian faith in particular. We hope through it to begin to answer some of those questions and to persuade people of the truth of the good news. Sometimes they come knowing little or nothing of the Christian message. Often they are confused and have many misunderstandings. Sometimes there are special circumstances which have brought them to the group, a family tragedy for instance; but most often they come because they have met Christians and they want to know more. Their lives have been touched and they are open to the message of the good news.

Such openness is much more common than we think. We have a natural tendency to assume a defensive attitude, being the minority group that we are. We consider the world to be against us, which it sometimes is, and we transfer this attitude to the individuals we meet. We will meet opportunities as we have already thought; but we will also discover a great openness to the gospel amongst our friends, especially if we learn to communicate it effectively.

When we were rethinking the role of the group within

our church life recently, we asked present and past members what were the things that they particularly valued about the group. A number of things were mentioned but perhaps the most important were the freedom to be able to question, the honesty of the leaders in admitting when they didn't know the answers and in talking about their own experience, and the time to be able to grasp the truths of the Christian message in an unhurried and unpressurised atmosphere. As we as individuals get involved in sharing the good news with others we will find that they too have many questions. We will also find that if we can learn to help them to find answers to those questions, and if we maintain an honesty and integrity in our approach to them, then our openness will very often be matched by an openness on their side as well.

I suppose that technically what we are talking about here would be described as 'Apologetics', just as what we have been talking about so far would be called 'Evangelism'. But what is apologetics? It comes from a Greek word *apologia*, which doesn't mean to apologise in our sense of the word. It means to provide a legal defence. There are many other words used in the Bible which are associated with the word *apologia*. There is the Greek word from which our word 'dialogue' comes, which means to argue; again, not in the sense of an angry dispute, but rather in the sense of presenting a reasoned case. Other words that would come under the heading would be translated 'refute', 'convince', 'persuade', 'plead' or 'prove'. All of them point to a presentation of a thought out case. That is what lies behind the whole thinking of apologetics. It is the presentation of a clearly thought out case for believing in God or believing in Jesus Christ. The *Oxford English Dictionary* defines an apologist as 'one who defends by argument'. It is one way, therefore, of communicating a message.

It is important for us at this juncture to see that this is the way that we are most likely to be involved in communicating the good news. For when we begin to engage in conversation with people about the good news it will not be

79

long before questions and objections are voiced. If we have not thought about those questions then we will come unstuck at the first hurdle. If we are to learn to communicate the good news effectively we need to learn to be 'apologists'. We probably won't want to use that word, just as we may not want to talk about ourselves as 'evangelists', but we will need to be able to present reasons for our faith which can stand up to scrutiny.

We may understand this a bit more clearly if we contrast and compare this means of communication with others. Broadly speaking there are three ways of trying to get a point across. One is proclamation, another is what we might call polemic and the other is apologetics. We can illustrate these three from the life of politics. Politicians use the art of proclamation. They love to make speeches. They stand up and present what they see to be a case in spoken form. They do it in the House of Commons; they do it at election time; they do it in many different ways. Secondly, politicians frequently use polemic, both in spoken and written form. The *Oxford English Dictionary* defines polemic as 'controversial discussion'. It often involves twisting what other people have said, or saying things about them which are only partly true – blowing up half of the truth so that it becomes considerably exaggerated. You only have to watch TV political discussions to see that politicians are up to this the whole time. They often take one of their opponent's phrases out of context and throw it back at them. This method is used mostly because people are concerned to win the argument at all costs. They don't care if their case is better than the other case or worse. All they are concerned about is winning the argument and therefore any method will do. But politicians also use apologetics. They tend not to use it quite so often when they are electioneering. It is mostly proclamation and polemic at election time; but at other times you find them reasoning a case, particularly with their own supporters when they are trying to persuade them of a particular viewpoint. They don't have to use polemic and they can't simply tell them; for they want to make sure that people understand. So they present a fair, balanced and reasoned argument.

The distinction, however, is not always clear-cut, because proclamation, for instance, can include both polemic and apologetics. For the Christian, however, polemic is clearly out. The only two methods of communication that are open to us are proclamation and apologetics; and both are used in the New Testament. Polemic is not. I was involved recently in a dialogue with some Muslims at their invitation. A Muslim speaker and I were both invited to speak to a mixed group on the subject of 'Repentance'. Following that we answered questions and then there followed a more informal time of discussion. I found myself talking later on in the evening with a Muslim man who, though he would have claimed that he was doing apologetics, was actually engaging in simple polemic. He would make broad, sweeping statements about the Christian case followed by statements about the Muslim case. When I asked 'What's the evidence? Why do you believe that?' he would say that there was lots of evidence. Yet every time we asked him for something specific, nothing was forthcoming. He was refusing to listen to what we were saying.

However, before we become too critical, we need to recognise that it can happen with Christians too. It can happen when we try to answer questions that people aren't asking, a very tempting thing to do. Politicians, again, do it all the time. They set up a question that nobody is asking, but which sounds good. They answer it and the answer sounds very good too. You are thinking to yourself what a clever answer it was, then afterwards you realise that it wasn't the answer to the real question at all. It is very easy for us to do that in presenting the Christian gospel, to set up a hypothetical question and answer it while avoiding the real question that was asked. It's easy too to make excessive claims on very slender evidence. I've often heard Christians doing this, and have caught myself doing it as well, building a case around one little piece of archaeological evidence or something which we have discovered. We've

81

read about it in a book. So we build a whole case on this one piece of evidence. As part of a cumulative case it may have value but on its own it is actually a fairly flimsy piece of evidence; yet a lot is built upon it. That is polemic and not apologetics. We are making our point but it is not a clear and well reasoned argument.

The silly thing is that for Christians it is not necessary to engage in those sorts of tactics; for there are plenty of good arguments and there is plenty of good evidence for our faith. What we need to learn to do, and this is what this second part of the book is really all about, is to find out what that evidence is and to learn to present answers to people's questions and objections in a clear and thought out manner. That is what apologetics is, the business of presenting reasoned and logical argument in order to persuade people of the truth. But why is this so important?

First let's look at the New Testament because, if it is important in the New Testament, it must be important for us. Of all those in the New Testament about whom we read, the two who are portrayed doing evangelism more than anybody else are Jesus and Paul. Both use many methods of communicating the good news, frequently engaging in apologetics. We often see Jesus in the Gospels in dialogue with his opponents or with people who are expressing interest. In John 8 for example we find the Jews having a discussion about who were the real children of Abraham and who were the children of Satan. Jesus enters into argument and discussion with them and shows them in a reasoned way that they are not really true children of Abraham, because they are not responding to his teaching. If we look in the first three Gospels, we find him being questioned about his use of the Sabbath or his attitude to the Law in general. In response we find him engaging in dialogue, in apologetics, explaining his reasons for why he healed people on the Sabbath. During the Sermon on the Mount, for instance, his explanation about his attitude to the Commandments is a form of apologetics.

Probably the greatest example, though, is in Mark 11 and

12. It makes a wonderful study to read through those chapters and watch Jesus at work. The events take place in the last week of his life. He is in Jerusalem and a number of groups come to him with different objections and questions. There is first of all the question of authority. The chief priests and the scribes come to him saying 'By what authority are you doing these things? Who gave you this authority to do them?' Jesus senses that their question is not a genuine question so he responds, as often happens in apolgetics, with another question back to them. He says 'I will ask you a question. Answer me and I will tell you by what authority I do these things. Was the baptism of John from heaven or from men? Answer me.' But, of course, for reasons of their own they weren't prepared to answer him; so he didn't answer them.

Then there was the question of paying taxes to Caesar. Again, they are trying to trap Jesus. But he responds with reasoned argument. He takes the coin which he gets them to offer to him, and asks 'Whose inscription is this?' He is able to turn the conversation, so that instead of them trapping him, they find themselves trapped by his argument and they are amazed at him. They wanted to know what he thought about Caesar. Jesus wanted to know what they thought about God. And Jesus certainly won that round of the argument.

Next comes the Sadducees' question. They try to trap him on the resurrection; but once again Jesus answers them, saying 'Is not this why you are wrong that you know neither the Scriptures not the power of God?' He goes on to show them the areas in which they are mistaken, giving examples from the Scriptures and pointing them to the reality of God's nature. We read at the end of the whole episode the telling sentence. 'After that no-one dared to ask him any questions.'

Jesus was the master of apologetics, of taking people's questions and seeing whether they were genuine or fraudulent. He was able not only to answer them but to turn their questions so that he not only dealt with their point, but also got across the point he was trying to make as well. It was an important method for him and if we are to be followers of his we need to learn to master this method of communication.

It was important, too, for Paul. There are many many passages we could turn to but chapters 17–19 of Acts makes a similarly fascinating study if we want to discover Paul's method of passing on the good news. We follow Paul on one of his missionary journeys and see what he did. We find him first of all in Thessalonica where Luke tells us that Paul went into the synagogue as was his custom and 'for three weeks he argued with them ® notice the word ⅜ from the Scriptures, explaining and proving that it was necessary for the Christ to suffer and rise from the dead and said "This Jesus whom I proclaim to you is the Christ".' And what happened? 'Some of them were persuaded and joined Paul and Silas as did a great many of the devout Greeks and not a few of the leading women.' They were persuaded. Paul argued; he presented a case; and they were persuaded.

Then we find him in Beroea and we read that there the Jews were more noble than those of Thessalonica for 'they received the Word with all eagerness, examining the Scriptures daily to see if these things were so'. Why did they examine the Scriptures? Because Paul must have taught them from the Scriptures. He presented the case; they went away to examine his case, to see if it held water, to see if it stood up to scrutiny. Moving on to Athens we find once again that 'he argued in the Synagogue with the Jews and the devout persons and in the market place every day with those who chanced to be there'. Following on from that we have recorded probably the greatest example of apologetics in the context of proclamation.

He comes next to Corinth. Many people argue from some of Paul's statements in his Corinthian letters that he gave up this method of arguing for his faith when he got to Corinth as he discovered in Athens that an intellectual approach didn't work. They argue that when he got to Corinth he went for a more simple approach and determined to know nothing except Jesus Christ and him crucified. They think that means that Paul gave up the kind of reasoned approach that he applied in Athens. But certainly Luke doesn't see it that way. When Paul gets to Corinth we find 'that he argued in the Synagogue every Sabbath and persuaded the Jews and Greeks'. His method hasn't changed at all. It is still his basic method to present his case clearly, in a reasoned and logical way. Thus when people are rising in opposition to Paul they say: 'This man is persuading men to worship God contrary to the Law.' They could see that was his method. He was persuading people.

There follows the very interesting example of

> a Jew named Apollos, a native of Alexandria who came to Ephesus. He was an eloquent man, well versed in the Scriptures. He had been instructed in the Way of the Lord; and being fervent in spirit, he spoke and taught accurately the things concerning Jesus, though he only knew the baptism of John. He began to speak boldly at the Synagogue; but when Priscilla and Aquila heard him, they took him and expounded to him the way of God more accurately. And when he wished to cross to Achaia, the brethren encouraged him and wrote to the disciples to receive him. When he arrived he greatly helped those who through grace had believed, for he powerfully confuted the Jews in public, showing by the Scriptures that the Christ was Jesus (Acts 18.24–28).

Do you notice that subtle shift there? In the first half of those verses he is speaking clearly, even accurately; but after he has been instructed more fully, he is able to confute the arguments of others. He is able not only to communicate himself, but also to take what is coming back and deal with it. He has gone a stage further on. He is involved now, not only in proclamation, but in apologetics as well.

Finally we find Paul back in Ephesus. Luke tells us again that 'he entered the Synagogue and for three months spoke boldly, arguing and pleading about the Kingdom of God. But when some were stubborn and disbelieved, speaking evil of the Way before the congregation, he withdrew from them taking the disciples with him and argued daily in the Hall of Tyrannus. This continued for two years so that all the residents of Asia heard the Word of the Lord, both Jews and Greeks (Act 19.8–10).

Once more Paul is portrayed arguing and pleading his case.

I hope that gives you some flavour of how important a part of the communication of the good news apologetics was in New Testament times, both for Jesus himself and also for Paul. Of course we need to remember that this is only one method. As Paul writes in Philippians, 'You are all partakers with me of grace, both in my imprisonment and in the defence and confirmation of the gospel.' He strikes a lovely balance, typical of Scripture, between the two parts of proclaiming the gospel, its defence and confirmation. (The word for defence there is once again *apologia*.) He is saying that there are two sides to the business of communicating the gospel. There is information people don't know that we need to communicate. There will be questons and objections that we must answer.

If this method of communicating the good news was important to Jesus and to Paul, it is no less important today; for people have an enormous number of questions. You have probably discovered this for yourself. I certainly have both through my own experience with friends and also through the Open to Question group. There are things people don't understand; there are things they object to; they want to know where the evidence is for what we believe. 'Why do you believe that?' 'Why do you accept Christianity as opposed to anything else?' 'How can you possibly believe in miracles?'

Furthermore, not only have we got to persuade people that Christianity is true, we also have to persuade them that Christianity is different from all the other varieties that are on offer. Most people have what I call a 'Pick 'n' Mix' mentality to religion. On the outside they want to say that they are interested to talk to us as we are Christians. But they may have another friend who is a Muslim. They want to examine the options, and then probably take a little bit of Christianity, a little bit of Islam, a bit of meditation from Buddhism and so on. Their aim is to create their own personal religion. Just as they wander down the sweet counter with a bag that they can fill according to their own desires, so they browse through the great religions of the world to create their own personalised variety.

In light of this Pick 'n' Mix mentality we have to give reasons for the exclusive claims of Christianity; for the exclusive nature of our faith is highly offensive to many people in our pluralistic society. We cannot simply tell people to believe, because they won't. We need to present reasons for why the Christian message we are wanting to put across is different from the other messages that are available. If the Church is to meet the world in its need we must have answers and reasons.

However, we also need to be aware of the danger of over-intellectualism. It is easy for us to believe that if we could only persuade people of the truth and get people convinced intellectually, then we would have achieved what we set out to achieve; and there's a danger that we will think that it can be done simply by argument. That is not true. We cannot rely simply on our own apologetic skills. If we say that communicating the gospel is simply an intellectual matter then we are missing out on a huge amount. There are other elements, aspects and perspectives that we need to bring into play.

I think of an occasion in Cambridge when I was talking with a young man and he asked me why I believed in the existence of God. I was about to plug into my 'this is the reason for believing in the existence of God' answer; not that I have the answer off pat, but I have a number of things which naturally and immediately spring into the front of my mind. I was about to start talking about creation, conscience and revelation in the person of Jesus, when suddenly something stopped me – I assume that God was giving me a nudge. Was that his real question? Was that actually what was going on in his mind or was it a question that he was putting forward as a smokescreen? It struck me that he was a deeply insecure person. From the whole way he was asking the question and from my previous knowledge of him I had a sense that that wasn't his need at all. What he was really wanting to know was whether there was any security to be found in believing in God. Could he really know that God loved him? So I answered his question but not along the lines I normally would at all, not along intellectual lines. Instead I started talking about God's love for him and of what I perceived to be his need for the love of God. As a result we got into a deeply personal conversation. We had actually touched base; we were talking about what really mattered to him. He did have real intellectual questions, but there was more to it than that.

On the other side we must also avoid the danger of anti-intellectualism. The New Testament sees us as whole people. It also sees the gospel as a whole package. The gospel has truth. It is intellectually true. It is intellectually fully supportable and believable. But also it is personally true, it is spiritually true. It meets our every need, the needs of our minds, our emotional needs, our psychological needs. It meets every need that we have. Because the gospel is a whole message the mind will always be involved; but it can never be only a matter for the mind. We will never get through to people without going through their minds; for if the gospel is the truth, there are facts that have got to be got across, that people have to understand; but there is more to it than that. However, within this overall perspective, the task of presenting a reasoned case for our faith is as urgent today as it has ever been.

But whose task is it to take on this work of arguing for our faith? It may be important but we may feel that we could never do it. However there are different levels at which this work is done. In one sense the answer to the question who is to do the work of apologetics is that all Christians are. Probably the most famous verse of all on apologetics is in 1 Peter 3.15. There Peter tells Christians, who were likely at any time to be called up before the authorities because of the fact that they were Christians, that they were always to be prepared to make a defence to anyone who called them to account for the hope that was in them. It is just the ordinary Christians to whom Peter is writing. Therefore we must conclude that in one sense, all Christians are to be able to give some sort of reasoned explanation as to why they believe what they believe.

Yet in another sense this work of apologetics is a special calling for people who are in positions of leadership. If we look at Titus 1.9 we discover that one of the qualifications for an overseer or elder or bishop is that he must 'hold firm to the sure Word as taught so that he may be able to give instruction in sound doctrine and also confute those who contradict him'. The balance appears again. He was to be able to explain the gospel clearly but he was also to be able to deal with people's objections, errors and questions. Similarly in 2 Timothy 4.2, Timothy, as one such elder or overseer, is told to 'preach the Word, to be urgent in season and out of season, to convince, rebuke and exhort, to be unfailing in patience and in teaching': again the positive and the negative sides of communication are there.

Just how we begin to get this balance in our presentation of the good news will be our subject in the chapters that follow. We will look first at the principles which need to govern our communication with others. We will look then at the most common questions that people ask.

9: The Meeting of Minds

Give a man a fish and you feed him for a day. Teach a man
to fish and you feed him and his family for life. Teach a
man to teach others to fish and you feed a village for ever.
In words similar to these TEAR fund presented their
philosophy of how to begin to meet world need. When I
was asked to write this book, I was asked specifically to deal
with some of the questions that have most frequently arisen
in our 'Open to Question' group. Though happy to do that
I wanted to make sure that we set these questions and any
possible answers within a right context. We have begun to
do that in Part One by looking at the area of the relationships in which these questions arise. They do not exist in a
vacuum. They come from real people. We have looked too
at the need to think through answers to people's questions,
to become 'apologists' for our faith. However before we
move on to think about some of the specific questions that
are frequently asked there is one more thing that we need to
do.

If there is to be the meeting of minds that is necessary for
communication to take place, then we need to understand
the principles that will make a meeting of minds possible.
Our aim is to communicate the message of the good news to
others; but we can only do that if the channels are open; and
by that I mean the channels in both directions. We need not
only to send the right messages but also to receive the right
messages as well. It would be possible for me simply to
write down some basic answers to the most common

questions that are asked. However if I were to do that and you were to learn them by heart, there would be little chance of any real communication taking place between you and those whose lives you touch. That is the way of the cults. They teach their pupils the answers – they give them a fish. We need to learn to think for ourselves about these issues – we need to learn to fish for ourselves, and even perhaps to be able to teach others to fish as well.

In this chapter therefore we will look at some general principles which apply to the answering of any questions that may arise; for in a book this size it would be impossible to deal with every question that might be asked; or even with every variation of one of the most common questions or objections. We will glean these principles once again from the example of Paul. We will take as our model his address to the Areopagus in Athens from Acts 17.16–34. If you don't know the passage it might be worth finding a Bible and reading it now before carrying on with this chapter. From it I want us to draw lessons about the three essential elements of effective communication.

The Preparation – Listening and Learning

This is essential to effective communication. If we fail to listen or to learn from what we hear we will never communicate effectively. If there is to be a genuine meeting of minds we need to understand what is going on in the mind of the person with whom we are speaking. We need to know not only what they are thinking but, as far as possible, why they are thinking it as well. We need to climb inside the non-Christian mind and try to see the world from their perspective. I have not yet seen the film *Crocodile Dundee* but I have heard so much about it that it is high on my list of films that I must see. I gather that the plot revolves around the meeting of the American journalist and a man from the Australian outback with no knowledge of modern civilisation. Each then in the course of the film introduces the other to 'their world'. We need a similar introduction to the non-Christian view of the world. This is especially important if we have been Christians for some time. The effect of spending most of our time with Christians is not only that we drift out of contact with the world; it is also that we find it much more difficult when we do touch the lives of others to be able to see things from their perspective.

This attitude of listening and learning is particularly important when it comes to answering people's questions about Christianity. It is so easy not to hear the real question. Though there are a number of questions that recur with great frequency, they always take a slightly different form. The differences may be subtle; they may not seem very important to us; but they may well be very important to the questioner. Take for instance the vexed question of suffering. Many times that question is asked as a general question. People look at the world; they see its suffering and they cannot understand how we can believe in a God of love. On other occasions, however, the question arises out of a particular circumstance, either in the life of the questioner or close to their immediate experience. Obviously the question needs to be approached with sensitivity regardless of the reason for which it has been asked. If, however, there is a particular tragedy that lies behind the question, the loss of a loved one, a broken relationship or whatever, then we will need to tread especially carefully. As I shall explain in the chapter on suffering later, there are certain things I would almost certainly omit from an an answer if I knew that person I was talking to was hurting badly at the time through some particular experience.

Furthermore, if we do not listen to their questions and comments, how can we expect them to listen to us? In the Muslim dialogue that I referred to in the last chapter, my attitude to the two people I dealt with was very different. The main speaker was a very gracious man. He listened to what I said; he listened to the questions that were asked from the floor; so I listened to him! The man I spoke to later was very different. There was an arrogance about him.

He treated what I had to say with contempt. As you can imagine I was not as receptive to what he had to say!

There are two common listening faults that I have experienced in talking to others about Jesus. The first is when we are not listening because we are too busy thinking about our own reply! It may sound silly but I would be surprised if you haven't found yourself in exactly that position – I certainly have. We need to realise that it is much more important to produce a response to what people are really saying, even if it is not very polished, than to give a wonderfully rounded and clever response to a point that they are not making. The second common failing is to listen, not so as to learn what our friends are thinking, but in order to put them in a pigeon-hole. We have an insatiable appetite for putting labels on people that we must resist strongly. We love, too, to label their questions – 'Ah, yes. That of course is a splendid example of the classic "Science contradicts Christianity" objection.' But people don't like being labelled or put into pigeon-holes. In a society which is growing increasingly impersonal we will only find a true openness in people if we treat them as individuals, with their own particular questions. From our point of view their questions may be classic examples of the old familiars; but from their point of view (which is the one that matters) they may be deeply held objections or questions that trouble them a great deal.

Listening may sound easy; but it needs to be worked at. I think of one of our leaders in the 'Open to Question' group. I can recall him on many occasions saying something like this: 'Let me tell you what I think you are saying.' (He would then explain what he had heard.) 'Before I respond to that, perhaps you could tell me if I've understood you correctly.' If the answer was 'No', he got them to repeat what they had said until he grasped the point that they were trying to make. Now Karl would be the first to admit that he has had to work at this. He is a politically active journalist who is used to putting across his own view forcefully. As a Christian seeking to communicate the good news he has learnt to listen and learn. As a result he is a very effective communicator of the Christian message.

Though listening is especially important in our relationships with individuals, we also need to cultivate an attitude which listens and learns from everything that goes on around us. We are all influenced to a very great extent by what we read, by the things we watch on television and by the thinking of our contemporary philosophers, playwrights and authors. We may not read them directly but their influence pervades our society. If we are to understand the thinking of our non-Christian friends we need to learn to listen to the undercurrents of thinking in our society. In our society there is very little acceptance of any absolutes. All things are seen to be relative. Is something right or wrong? It depends on the circumstances, we are told. Is something true or false? That too depends on what you mean by truth. According to our society something can be true for one person but not for another. In other words truth is measured and assessed according to whether it works, not by any absolute standard. In such a framework our message which concerns Jesus who is the Truth, which involves a morality based on absolutes, is bound to run into opposition and misunderstanding. To cope with that it is essential that we see why our friends find our message so foreign to their way of thinking.

I said at the beginning of this chapter that we were going to look at Paul as our model. In Acts 17 we see that this principle of listening and learning was an essential part of his preparation. 'Men of Athens', he says, 'I perceived [note the word] that you are very religious. For as I passed along, and observed [visual listening] the objects of your worship . . .' Later in the same passage he quotes to them the work of their own poets. He understood the way they thought because he had kept his ears and eyes open and had learnt from what he had observed.

The Style – Constructive not Confrontational

If Paul's work was marked by thorough preparation, it was also done in a style that was constructive and not confrontational. Our aim after all is to win the person and not the argument. On the occasion of the Muslim dialogue I remember my rector, Richard Bewes, praying beforehand that I would not lose my temper! I learnt afterwards that his reason for praying that prayer was because he had had to deal all evening with the man I have described, when he had taken part in a similar session the fortnight before. He had experienced the confrontational style of the man and he knew that it would be destructive for me to enter into that spirit.

Occasionally we will need to confront people with the need to decide or to face up to the truth. However it should be something we keep in reserve and only use when we have a well established relationship with someone. Generally we will want to imitate the constructive style of Jesus and of Paul. But what will that mean?

It will mean controlling our feelings. Luke tells us that when Paul saw the idols of Athens 'his spirit was provoked within him.' It's instructive to note that when Paul was a tourist in Athens he did not marvel at their architectural expertise. Rather he was angered by their rejection of the living God and by their worship of worthless idols. However he does not let that anger show. It must have motivated him very strongly but he controlled those feelings of anger, channelling them into constructive ways. There is no direct rebuke to the Athenians. There is forthright exposure of error but it is done in a controlled manner. We may well meet aggressive responses to some of the things we say. It is a mistake to respond with aggression. We too need to channel our feelings in constructive and helpful directions.

It will mean that we will be keener to point to the truth than to concentrate on their errors. As Paul puts it, 'The times of ignorance God overlooked, but now he commands all men everywhere to repent, because he has fixed a day on which he will judge the world.' He is much more concerned with the present and the future than with the past. Similarly, though their beliefs were full of errors, he does not rub their noses in the folly of their ways but uses their thinking as a contrast to the truth that he is trying to put across. Often people will make statements or voice objections to us which are so full of error or misunderstanding that we will not know where to begin. We could respond by pointing out their errors one by one; but that would not be very constructive. Alternatively we could either begin with one such error and move from it to its corresponding truth or, perhaps better still, find some element of truth in what they have said and seek to build on that.

Our aim always needs to be to get back to the gospel, for that is where the power lies. We need to answer the questions that people have; but ultimately their minds and wills will only be moved by the power of the gospel. I was told early in my Christian life to have going round in the back of my mind all the time I was seeking to talk to others about the gospel the phrase 'Get back to Jesus, get back to Jesus'. This is no cop-out. It is not avoiding the question; for in the end every question finds its answer in Jesus, as we shall see in the chapters that follow. One of the key skills that we must learn is how to turn a conversation away from the blind alleyways that we are often led into and back to the person of Jesus Christ.

A constructive approach will also mean that we will be honest and caring — honest in our admission that we don't know all the answers, caring in our concern for the person, not just for their arguments. We are not in a confrontation. Though there is a spiritual battle taking place, the person to whom we are speaking is the captive not the enemy. They are much more likely to be impressed by our honesty in admitting that we don't know the answer to a particular question than by an insubstantial answer that we try to defend even though it is obviously incomplete. I love John

Chapman's dictum that the time when we don't know the answer is an opportunity not a problem. We see it as a problem because, for some strange reason, we are labouring under the illusion that we are or should be infallible! In reality, says Chappo, it is an opportunity; for we are then able to say to our friend 'I'm sorry but I don't know the answer to that question. I'll have to go and find it out. When I've done a bit of work on it we can talk again.' The door is left open. We can then do some study of our own or ask an older Christian friend or minister to discover an answer. A seeming disaster has become an opportunity for us to learn and for a further conversation with our friend.

This does not mean that we should become wishy-washy or insipid. You could hardly say that about the words of Paul concerning repentance and judgement quoted above. It does mean that our style should be marked and governed by a desire to build and not destroy. It is much easier to destroy than to build, to criticise than to see the good. We will often be met by critical and destructive attitudes as we seek to communicate the good news. We need therefore to be on our guard that we do not respond in a similar vein.

The Content – Relevant and Well-Reasoned

Paul's address to the Athenians could not have been more relevant to them. He started 'where they were'. However he then built on that and the ground that they shared in common to present a case which is remarkable for its simple yet profound logic. He tells them that 'the God who made the world and everything in it, being Lord of heaven and earth, does not live in shrines made by man'. As soon as it is put in those terms the absurdity of seeing any man-made temple or building as the house of God is exposed. So too are all attempts to limit God as people do today by putting him in an intellectual box – 'I can't believe in a God who would send anyone to hell.' We fail to see that what we can or can't believe is not the issue; for we are dealing with the Creator. He makes the rules, not us.

97

Paul goes on 'nor is he served by human hands, as though he needed anything, since he himself gives to all men life and breath and everything'. The Athenians thought that their gods needed them. Paul pictures their sacrifices as a form of heavenly meals-on-wheels service for the poor gods who can't manage on their own any more. Such thinking is of course absurd when we see that God is not only the Creator but also the Sustainer of the universe. He doesn't need us. We need him. You would never guess that from the way that many people approach him today. There is an air of condescension about them as if God would be very lucky if they chose to join his team. The reality is very different.

Towards the end of his address, following a quotation from the Athenians' own poets, Paul comments: 'Being then God's offspring, we ought not to think that the Deity is like gold, or silver, or stone, a representation by the art and imagination of man.' The logic is once again unanswerable. If we come from God, how can he be expressed either in inanimate terms or even by any concept from our imagination. He must be greater than us not less than us. He must by definition be beyond our imagination.

Notice that in each of these examples there is the balance between the positive and the negative that we were thinking about in the last chapter. He deliberately and effectively undermines the foundations of their thinking and beliefs, while at the same time imparting a greal deal of positive information about the true nature of God. His address also finishes exactly where Paul wants it to, on the person of Jesus. Part of our task also is to undermine the thinking of those we meet. From their viewpoint we are seen as those standing in quicksand or leaning on a non-existent crutch. By their questions and objections they are trying to show us that. Their hidden assumption is that they are standing on the rock-solid ground of human reason. Nothing of course could be further from the truth; for in reality the ground that we are standing upon is much more solid than theirs. In the first place we need to remember that ourselves so that we are not thrown by their questions; but we also need to point it out to them as well, for we are wanting them to do nothing less than shift the whole foundation of their lives. In order to take that decision, they need not only to see that what we are proposing is solid and will hold them up, but also to understand that their current foundations are much more shaky than they realise.

However, if we are to communicate effectively on either the positive or the negative level, our reasoning must be good; and, in particular, it must be acceptable to the person to whom we are speaking. What is good reasoning to one person may not be to another for they may not accept some of the assumptions on which it is based. There are a number of questions that we need to ask of any answer that we give. Is the argument I'm using relevant to the person to whom I am speaking? Do they accept the logic which is the basis of my point? If not, have I justified my use of that logic? That may sound complicated but it is obvious when we put it into a concrete example. Take for instance the reliability of the Bible. To someone who believes in God, and that Jesus is his Son, we can argue that Jesus' attitude to the Old Testament shows that he accepted it as God's Word; and that therefore we ought to accept it as such as well. To someone who does not believe in God at all, such an argument is nonsense and we will need to start from a point much further back.

It is perfectly reasonable, though, to build a cumulative case and ask people to make certain assumptions along the way, not asking them to accept them necessarily but to try to see what difference it would make if they did. As long as this is recognised on both sides it is a very helpful way of proceeding. I find, for example, that I often need at the outset to try and broaden people's horizons. Their thinking is like most of ours, narrow and self-centred. In that case I use an illustration which I have found very helpful. Before the arrival of Copernicus, scientists of those days believed that the earth was the centre of the universe. They explained the movement of the sun and the planets in terms of some highly complex shapes with elaborate curls and gyrations. However, as soon as Copernicus persuaded them to change their one basic assumption, that the earth was the centre of the universe, to the assumption that the sun was at the centre, it all became much easier to explain. Suddenly the picture became much clearer, the orbits of the planets became simple elipses rather than the extraordinary shapes that they had had to invent in order to fit their basic assumption. Similarly many people assume that we are at the centre of life and God, if he exists, is at the circumference. We need to persuade them to see that in reality God is at the centre and we are at the circumference.

Another general illustration that I use to make a similar point concerns a judge and the person in the dock. From the way in which many approach God it seems that they view themselves as being in the judgement seat with God in the dock. They are deciding whether or not to accept him. As soon as we put in in those terms the absurdity becomes obvious; for, if God is God, then he is in the judgement seat and we are in the dock. The real question is not 'What shall I do with him?' but 'What will he do with me?'

With these principles in mind we can move on to look at some of the common questions that people ask. However, as we do so, I would ask you to treat the material that follows not as a fixed structure but as bricks and cement which you can put together in many different ways according to the need of the moment and the perspective of the particular person to whom you are talking. I am tempted to put a Government Health Warning at the top of each chapter saying 'Danger: pat answers can be a serious obstacle to effective communication'; but I will resist such temptation while urging you to take the warning on board. We would all love to become experts at communicating the good news overnight, but it doesn't happen that way. It takes time. We will make mistakes. The important thing is to keep listening and learning, to seek to build and not destroy and to work at being relevant and well-reasoned in what we say. If we do these things then there will be a meeting of minds and effective communication will begin. Hopefully the chapters that follow will help that process.

10: Is There a God?

There's no place to start like the beginning! This is of course the most fundamental question of all. However, before we look at it, we must provide ourselves with a framework. For each question we need to see first what the common objections are; then we need to get a right expectation of what point we want to get people to; and finally we have to decide what are the relevant arguments and pieces of evidence.

In this particular case the questions and objections that fall under this general heading are many; but for most the question is not whether or not God exists. A recent opinion poll found that 80% of people in Britain were prepared to say that they believed in the existence of God. I suspect that in reality the percentage is higher than that. In experience there are very few true atheists. However the question does arise in the form at the heading of this chapter. More often, though, it appears in other ways. Many would be unsure of the nature or character of God. They believe in a Power that is greater than us, but whether that Power is personal or impersonal, good or evil, they are unsure. They want to know if there is any way in which they can know what God is like. Others want to know what God is doing; they see little evidence of his activity in the world. Some couldn't care less if there is a God or not; he seems irrelevant to them. Others again think in more experiential terms – 'God hasn't spoken to me. When he does I'll believe in him.'

We can see from the variety above that this question takes

a number of different forms. Where we begin and what we concentrate on will depend very much on the particular form of the question. Before looking at the issue raised by these questions, we must consider how far we might reasonably expect to take someone in their thinking, for whom this is their fundamental question. If someone is questioning the very existence of God it is unlikely that we will persuade them in the course of one conversation to commit themselves to Christ. If we make that our expectation we are likely to be disappointed. If instead we set ourselves the target of getting them at least to allow for the possibility of there being a God, or better still to begin to look actively at the evidence for his existence, then we are much more likely to achieve what we set out to do. If on the other hand they already believe in God but are unsure of his nature we might have a higher expectation. We might aim for instance to persuade them to read one of the Gospels, to look at the person of Jesus in order to see who they think that he is.

This may sound like defeatist talk – surely our aim is to win people for Christ. Yes it is; but for most people it is a process. There are many steps on the road from unbelief to faith. If we can help our friends to take one or two steps along that road at any one time then we are making progress. If our expectations are too high of how quick that progress will be then we will be very disappointed and may well give up.

In seeking to answer any of these questions there are three main areas that we might explore. Where we start and how far we go would depend as we have already thought on the starting point of the questioner. It would be rare to use all of this material in one answer. The areas that concern us here are, first of all, the nature of proof, then the principle of revelation and lastly the content of that revelation.

The Nature of Proof

'Prove to me the existence of God.' A common request, but

what is proof? Normally such a request is based upon a materialistic view of the world – 'Unless I can see it, or touch it, or feel it, I can't believe in it.' Such questioners are looking for what they see to be a scientific proof. An interesting question to ask in return is to set them a test. Ask them to prove to you three things that you both accept as facts from different areas of life. Take, say, the law of gravity, the life of Queen Elizabeth I and the fact that I love my wife.

The first fact is provable by scientific experiment. If someone drops an apple above my head, it will always fall on my head. By repeating this experiment again and again we find that on the earth it is a law, a fact. The life of Queen Elizabeth I is a slightly different type of fact. If you were to go into any history faculty in a college or university, and suggest that she never lived, you would be laughed out of court! But I can't touch her; I can't see her; I can't do experiments on her. There is a vast mass of evidence for her existence but it is historical evidence not experimental or scientific evidence. The evidence takes the form of documents and papers, of pictures and buildings. Her life is a fact but the evidence is of a very different form. The third fact is even more of an enigma. I know it to be fact. My wife does not know it in the absolute sense of that word; but she believes it. Why? Partly on the evidence of what I say to her, partly by the way I treat her, partly through what she feels within herself as she senses that her love for me is reciprocated. It's a much more difficult fact to establish; but to my wife and me it is much more important than the life of Elizabeth I, even though we both studied history at one time!

In reality none of these proofs is watertight. The world we live in is complex. There are, however, important similarities and differences between them. All are based on evidence. That evidence takes different forms but it is a common factor. Furthermore all evidence is at least largely, if not completely, a matter of observation. The differences lie in the form of the evidence and the nature of the proofs. For different facts different types of evidence are relevant, scientific evidence for scientific facts, historical evidence for historical facts and personal evidence for personal facts. The type of evidence dictates the nature of the proof.

If we apply this to the question of the existence or nature of God, then it must be clear that we cannot provide a scientific proof for his existence. There is however plenty of historical and personal evidence for his existence. Whether it amounts to a proof depends on the individual who examines it, as it does with any other form of proof. In a legal trial before a jury the twelve men and women, good and true, have to examine the evidence and decide whether or not the case is proven. Our task when people question the existence or nature of God is to show them that there is evidence and to get them to examine it for themselves. In doing so they will need to take on board the fact that in dealing with this question we are going into unknown territory; we cannot simply apply methods and concepts to the question of God's existence that we apply, say, to the question of Queen Elizabeth I's existence. This brings us on to the second area that we might explore when answering this question.

The Principle of Revelation

The illustration of the judge and the man in the dock from the last chapter shows the reality of our position before God. If God exists he must by definition be greater than we are. We must not imagine, therefore, that we can think our way to understanding him. If we could, we would be God; and he would be our creature. How then can we know anything about God? The answer of Christian, Jew and Muslim alike is that we can only know about God what he chooses to reveal to us. This is surely an undeniable propostion if God exists. If he doesn't, there is of course nothing to be revealed and no one to reveal it. The consequence of this, however, which is what concerns us in this context, is that any evidence for God's existence will be provided by God himself. This puts it into a category all of its own. Part of the evidence takes an historical form but even then it is unique within that type. Normally evidence needs to be checked against another authority or, in scientific terms, against a control experiment. However, though some of the evidence for God's existence and character is of a type that can be corroborated, it has an essential quality about it because there is, and never could be, a higher authority or even a parallel authority who could authenticate it.

In practice this means that there is bound to be a certain circularity in some of the arguments which we will use to defend our faith. It means too that we will have to show people that the proof to look for is not one that stems from an outside or greater authority, but that which comes from an integral consistency. That is one of the key things to get people to look for. The argument may be circular but is there any flaw or break in the circle? If not, does not the very perfection of the circle point to the truth of the assumption on which it is based?

The Content of Revelation

All of this is getting perhaps a little too theoretical. It's time to examine what evidence God has provided. Broadly speaking his revelation of himself is normally seen to be in two categories, general revelation, that is, what can be seen or experienced by all people, and special or specific revelation, that is, revelation which comes to certain people at particular times and in particular places. Creation would be an example of the former and God's dealings with the people of Israel an example of the latter. As far as general revelation is concerned there are two main pieces of evidence which point to God's existence: creation and conscience.

The order of creation has long been an argument for God's existence. Paul himself used it in Romans 1.19–20.

'For what can be known about God is plain to them, because God has shown it to them. Ever since the creation of the world his invisible nature, namely, his eternal power and deity, has been clearly perceived in the things that have been made.' We will look in a later chapter at the supposed conflict between creation and evolution. For the moment we must notice both the strength and the limitation of this argument. The watch analogy has often been used, perhaps because it is helpful! As I look at the watch on my wrist I see order; I see a number of parts which have been put together. I could conclude that they came together by chance; or I could conclude that their order means that there must be a watchmaker who put them together, that such order could never have come about by chance. In the same way I look at the world and its order and conclude that there must be a Maker. However I can conclude little more than that; for though creation is strong evidence for the existence of God it tells me little about him except that he is great and powerful, just the points that Paul makes. It does not tell me for instance whether he is good or evil, personal or impersonal, a God of love or of hate.

Conscience, on the other hand, though potentially a more tricky subject, does point not only to God's existence but also to his goodness. Our ability to distinguish right from wrong has fascinated and puzzled philosophers for centuries. The explanation of this ability has been one of the key factors by which different philosophers have risen and fallen. If they cannot provide a satisfactory explanation then they die. Perhaps that is why philosophy continues to search for answers, because no human answer has proved acceptable; no human answer has explained the depth of this ability, emotion, call it what you will. However, alongside this struggle for a human answer, there has been the consistent testimony of those who believe in God that he is the explanation, that the reason we distinguish good from evil is because we are made in his image, we bear his stamp, we share some of his characteristics.

Neither of these two pieces of evidence constitutes a proof; but as part of a cumulative case they are useful building bricks. In any answer I would not normally reckon to spend too much time dealing with them because they can easily lead into blind alleys and much confusion – not least on our part! Instead I would move on to more firm evidence from the realm of special revelation, and in particular to the life of Christ.

The key question for anyone to answer is 'Who is Jesus Christ?' If he is God, then it is fairly logical to conclude that God exists. If he is God, then he can show us more of what God is like than anyone else. And that is who he claimed to be and what he claimed to be doing. Our whole case rests or falls on Jesus and on his claims. 'He who has seen me has seen the Father' (John 14.9). 'I am the way, the truth and the life. No one comes to the Father, but by me' (John 14.6). These are staggering claims and they come again and again in the Gospels and are repeated by the apostles. The question is whether they are true. To discover that, people need to look at the evidence for themselves, to read one of the Gospels, to read books about Jesus. This should be one of our main aims in talking to our friends. Ultimately we cannot force them to believe. They must be convinced of the tuth of the claims of Jesus and prepared to submit to him as Lord.

Much of the evidence for the truth of Jesus' claims comes in the chapters that follow: his death and resurrection, his uniqueness, and so on. However, one aspect which will probably not come again is the evidence of his character. To see this it is vital to look at the Gospels. The portrait of Jesus there portrayed is without parallel, the perfect balance he displays, his ability to deal with all manner and types of people. There is the astonishing fact that not only his disciples but also his family come to acknowledge him as the perfect Son of God. I like to think that my family have some respect for me; but I am under no illusion about what they would say if anyone tried to portray me as being perfect. Story after story would emerge of unkind words, bad temper and selfishness. In Jesus' case no such stories emerge. His family, his mother and his brothers, come not only to respect him but to worship him as God. There must have been something very remarkable about his character.

It was C.S. Lewis who said that we have only three possible choices concerning our answer to the question 'Who is Jesus?' Either he was who he claimed to be, God himself, or he was mad, or he was bad, an evil con man seeking to lead people astray for personal gain. Many people today would want to choose a fourth option, namely, that he was a good man and a remarkable teacher. In light of the evidence of his claims, which are not just added on to the New Testament record but which are woven inextricably into its very fabric, that is the one answer that is totally untenable. People hold it because they haven't looked at the evidence at first hand for such a long time. In light of that evidence it is difficult, too, to conclude that he was mad or bad. He had nothing to gain personally, especially from his avoidable death on the cross; and if he was mad, I suspect that many of us wish that there was more of that sort of madness in the world today.

There is, of course, also the evidence of our own experience of God. On its own it is subjective and can easily be written off as we have already thought. As part of the cumulative case it has a real role to play for it brings the whole matter into the realm of the personal, away from the theoretical and philosophical in which we can so easily become bogged down.

However, if time is short, or if we sense that we will only be able to get one point across in answer to any question about God's existence or character, then it must be Jesus that we talk about; and it must be the question 'Who do you think Jesus is?' that we leave with them. Even if we feel that it would be beneficial to show the person concerned that there are broader reasons for believing in God and that the case for God is philosophically sound, I would want always to finish by talking about Jesus; for not only is he the fullest answer that we have to any question about God, but also it is the message about him which is God's power for salvation.

108

11: Can I Trust The Bible?

As soon as we begin to get involved in any form of dialogue we are bound to face this question in one form or another. Whether we quote directly from the Bible or not, it will be quite clear that our case is heavily dependent on its reliability. There is no point therefore in trying to avoid the question by not using the Bible in our answers to other questions, though we will obviously want to avoid the danger of people thinking that we are hitting them over the head with it!

If we begin again by looking at the different forms that this question takes, we discover that again there are many. There is the fundamental question of its reliability – Can I believe what it says? But this is broken down into many more particular questions and objections:

The twenty or thirty years between the Gospel events and their being written down means that they must have been exaggerated.

The writers were biased and therefore we can't believe what they say.

Many Christians today don't accept the Bible as literally true.

With so many different interpretations how can we know what it really means anyway?

It's full of contradictions.

How can a book written 2,000 years ago possibly be relevant to me today?

The Old Testament is about a different God from the New. The Old Testament God is a harsh judge. The New speaks of a God of love.

I wonder how many of these questions or objections you have come across, or how many others you could add to the list. In light of such a barrage of questions it is important both that we have a right idea of what we expect the outsider to believe about the Bible, and also that we have a clear framework for our thinking about the subject. Remember that we are dealing in these chapters not with answers that we can repeat but with pointers that can help us to get our thinking clear. On this and other subjects you may well need to follow up the thinking here in other books.

My expectation is very simple when talking with people about the Bible. I would not dream of trying to persuade an outsider that the Bible was the Word of God and utterly reliable. I believe that myself; but my belief is based on a number of assumptions about Jesus and about the nature of God that I would not expect the outsider to share. If he did I would ask him to commit himself to Christ then and there, because he would have no good reason not to. Our aim surely is to get the outsider to take the Bible seriously, to recognise its remarkable historical standing amongst literature of the time, so that he will read it. If we spend ages trying to prove the inspiration of Scripture we will end up tying ourselves in knots. A much more profitable expectation is to get people to accept that the New Testament is a reasonably reliable record of what Jesus said and did and of what the early Christians believed about him. Understanding the full beauty and authority of the Bible can come later. Notice, too, that I say the New Testament. Though I firmly believe that the Old Testament speaks of the same God as the New, I would not want to spend too much time trying to show that. My aim is always that people will look afresh at Jesus Christ. I want them, therefore, to read a Gospel, and to be able to read it knowing that there are good reasons for treating it as a remarkable historical document.

With that in mind we have narrowed the field somewhat. We don't have to learn how to explain the different theories of inspiration! But where do we start to get our thinking straight? There are two basic questions that we must ask. First, can we be sure that what we have in our Bibles is what the original authors wrote or has it been tampered with as it has been copied through the ages? Secondly, 'is what they wrote true', and, 'can we trust them as accurate historians?'

Do We Have What They Originally Wrote?

Of the two questions this is the more straightforward for there is very strong evidence that, barring a few small discrepancies, the New Testament that we have today is a very accurate copy of what was originally written. Our reasons for believing this are largely based on comparing the New Testament with other historical documents of the time. There are two key tests of the authenticity of ancient documents. First, how near in time to the writing of the original is the date of the first complete copy that we have? Second, how many copies do we have that date from that time? You may wonder why we don't have the originals themselves. The answer is that we have almost no original documents from that time as they were made of a material that did not last very long. This was clearly understood by all keepers of documents and was catered for by professional copiers who made accurate copies and then often destroyed the originals. This was done because the originals were deemed to be more likely to be corrupted through decay than the new copy through errors in copying. Josh McDowell records in his book *Evidence that Demands a Verdict* a list of the stringent conditions that were laid down for those who copied the Old Testament Scriptures.

The fact therefore that we have complete copies of the New

Testament which date back to *AD* 240 to 250 may not sound very impressive, a gap of 200 years from the time that they were written. However, when we add to that that we have fragments of the Gospels which go back more than 100 years before that, and when we begin to compare these figures with comparable figures concerning other well-known documents from the time, then the picture changes. Figure 1 shows a comparison between the New Testament and two other contemporary documents.

Document	Date written	Earliest copy	Gap (yrs)	Number of copies
Tacitus' Annals	100 AD	1100 AD	1000	20
Caesar's Gallic Wars	60 BC	900 AD	960	10
The New Testament	50–70 AD	130 AD	60	A fragment
		400 AD	330	Many

[Figure 1]

No ancient historian seriously doubts the fact that what we read today as Tacitus' *Annals* or Caesar's *Gallic Wars* are largely accurate copies of what Tacitus and Caesar wrote. If that is so we can be very confident that what we read in the New Testament is what the apostles originally wrote. Not only does the very short timespan between the originals and the first complete copy lead us to believe this, but the number of copies is also significant. Coming as they do from different parts of the world, and being very nearly identical, they show that they must have come from a common source some considerable time before. The greater the number of copies the further back that original must be.

However, we must be careful what we do and do not draw as conclusions from this evidence. It is strong evidence when produced to answer our first question, but it has little or nothing to say about our second question. It merely shows that when we read the New Testament we can be sure that what we have in front of us is in very large measure what was originally written. To take the example of Caesar's *Gallic*

Wars, for instance: it is commonly recognised that Caesar's account is considerably exaggerated and biased. He wrote it largely about himself! Needless to say he is shown in a very favourable light! To answer our second question we need different arguments.

Is What They Wrote an Accurate Record?

This question is much more difficult to answer; for it is not a matter of fact but of judgement. Whenever someone tells us something, we have to make a judgement. Is it true or false or just a mild exaggeration? Some people are compulsive liars. Others love to embroider stories with little extra details. Some people you know are utterly reliable. If they tell you something you know it's true, that that's exactly what happened and how it happened. Into which category do the writers of the New Testament fall? Clearly we cannot pretend that they were unbiased. Many of them tell us that they write for a specific purpose. 'These are written that you may believe that Jesus is the Christ, the Son of God, and that believing you may have life in his name' (John 20.31). 'Inasmuch as many have undertaken to compile a narrative of the things which have been accomplished among us, just as they were delivered to us by those who from the beginning were eyewitnesses and ministers of the word, it seemed good to me also, having followed all things closely for some time past, to write an orderly account for you, most excellent Theophilus, that you may know the truth concerning the things of which you have been informed' (Luke 1.1–4).

Bias is however no necessary barrier to accuracy. Accuracy depends on principles and method. The principles of the early Christians are clear. They believed their story to be true and they believed that truth was very important. That is clear from Luke's introduction above and from many other passages. In 1 Corinthians 15 when Paul is giving evidence for the resurrection of Jesus, he makes it plain that, if the resurrection never took place, our faith is futile and we are still in our sins. In fact he goes further: 'If for this life only we have hoped in Christ, we are of all men most to be pitied.' There are many other examples of the importance of truth to the early Christians, perhaps especially from the moral teaching of the New Testament on truthfulness and falsehood. It is ironic that our concern for the truth today, which stems out of the Christian roots of our society, should be used as an argument against Christianity; that we can't trust its foundation document!

The fact that the early Christians were prepared to die for what they believed is further evidence of the fact that they believed it to be true. If they had not been certain of that then they would have recanted under pressure; but they didn't and thousands died for their faith as a result. This, together with what we have seen above, is clear evidence that the early Christians believed that their message was true. But was it? Were they mistaken? Had they been fooled?

We saw above that accuracy depends on principles and method. Principles are subjective and therefore difficult to verify in any absolute way. Every indication from the New Testament is that the disciples were men and women of high principles and with a high regard for the truth. However we cannot produce any external evidence to back that up. The evidence comes from the book that we are seeking to verify. This is a clear example of the circularity that we were thinking about in the last chapter. We need to acknowledge this; but we also need to get people to ask whether or not they see an internal consistency and integrity in the New Testament evidence. When we move on to look at their method we are on different ground. Here we do have external evidence.

Luke claims that he 'followed all things closely for some time'. For many years he was accepted as one of the remarkable historians of ancient times; but then it became fashionable to ridicule Luke as an historian. It came to be believed that his supposed concern for detail could be shown to be highly inaccurate. We were told that the names and places which he mentions do not tie up with other sources, and so on. However as time has passed and as we learn more in particular from archaeology, Luke's reputation is fast

114

being restored even amongst those who were his critics. A classic example concerned his record that Quirinius was Governor of Syria at the time of the birth of Jesus. When it was discovered that Quirinius had been governor considerably later than the birth of Jesus, it was said that Luke was inaccurate. However, more recent discoveries have shown that there was a Quirinius who was governor of Syria at an earlier stage, which would be consistent with Luke's account. Whether it was the same Quirinius or another we do not know.

There is an arrogance today which assumes we can know more now of what happened then than those writing at the time. There are unanswered questions concerning apparent contradictions within the New Testament and concerning various pieces of archeological evidence. However, both because of what I see of the character of the New Testament writers in their writings, and also because of the body of evidence that supports the accuracy of the New Testament, I would want to put forward a strong case for the New Testament's being a truthful account of what the disciples of Jesus saw and heard.

There is other external evidence in the writings of Tacitus, the Roman historian, and Josephus, the Jewish historian. They both refer to Jesus and to the phenomenon of the early Church. However their references are sketchy and they add no significant detail to the New Testament account. This is one example of how easy it is to clutch at straws or to try and build too much on slender evidence. As part of the cumulative case for the New Testament the references in Tacitus and Josephus have something to contribute; but on their own they show us very little, except that Christian beliefs were being talked about in Jewish and Roman circles in the first century AD.

But what of the time delay betwen the events and their being recorded? How could the disciples possibly remember what Jesus had said twenty-five or thirty years before? If we go back twenty-five or thirty years from today, we come to the period of the late 50s and early 60s. The events from those days which stick in my mind, even though I was still in single figures in those days, are the first manned space flight and the assassination of President Kennedy. I can remember them both vividly and where I was when I was told about them. For the former I was playing in front of our house with other children from the neighbourhood on a large expanse of green. For the latter I remember a game of gym football being interrupted at school when someone came in to tell us. The main events of Jesus' life would have stuck very firmly in the minds of the disciples both because they would have been so important to them and also becuase they formed part of what they taught day by day in the early Church. It isn't as if there was a gap when the subject wasn't mentioned, and then thirty years later a reporter turned up and said: 'I wonder if you remember a man called Jesus. Can you tell me anything about him?'

Furthermore, memory played a much more important part in the life of those days than it does today. These days we don't need to remember things so much because we have so many memory aids, the written word, television and radio archives and so forth. In those days, when many were illiterate, memory played a much more important part. It is known that the human brain adapts and only develops at a given time those abilities which are really needed. For instance, I used to be very quick at mental arithmetic. I would pride myself on working out sums at great speed with no pencil and paper and of course without a calculator, which was then an expensive and rare item. Nowadays I have several calculators and my powers of mental arithmetic are much less because I hardly ever use them. Similarly today we memorise very little. In those days, however, memorising things was one of the main ways of passing on information and was a common method used by teachers. It is highly likely, to take one example, that Jesus taught the disciples the Sermon on the Mount over a period of a few days, getting them to memorise the essentials, which he would then have expanded upon. The time delay of twenty-five or thirty years is not really very significant at all.

One of the main reasons that it was not all written down before is that they believed that Jesus' return was imminent. When it became clear that Jesus might not be returning in their lifetime, they made sure that the evidence of the original eye-witnesses, of whom Luke speaks, was written down for future generations and for use by missionaries. Until that time there was little need for complete accounts (there were almost certainly some written records that preceded the Gospels) because the eyewitnesses were still around to speak for themselves.

The above is by no means a complete answer to the questions with which we began; but I hope it gives a framework and some more building bricks which we can use. A friend of mine studied at Cambridge for four years, first studying Classics, including a fair amount of Ancient History, and then moving on to study Theology. The contrast he found between the lecturers in the two university departments was most extraordinary. In the Classics Department they treasured every document they possessed; for in any given subject there were not many around. Yes, they looked at them critically and questioned their accuracy and authenticity. However, underlying that was an attitude of respect. When he moved to the Theology faculty he discovered near contempt for a group of documents that most of his Classics teachers would have given their eye teeth to possess as they were so remarkably well attested. Untold damage has been done to the credibility of the New Testament by many within the Church, and often for little good reason.

The documents we possess in the New Testament are remarkable historical documents, written by a courageous group of people, who believed so firmly that their message was true that they were prepared to die rather than deny it. We can present this book to any enquirer with confidence, not seeking to persuade them that it is the Word of God, though we may well believe that, but offering it to them as the central source of evidence for the Christian faith; for after all our aim is that they should read it for themselves and, as John says, that they should 'believe that Jesus is the Christ, the Son of God, and that believing they might find life in his name'.

117

12: Don't All Religions Lead to God?

In light of the exclusive claims of Christianity this question is almost bound to arise. Closely allied to it is the question: 'What about those who have never heard of Jesus?' Its form varies less than some of the other questions because of the nature of the question. However the angle from which people are approaching it can be very different. For some it is a personal question because they come from another religious tradition. The claims of Christianity, therefore, are a personal affront to them. For others it is a more general principle that worries them. They have been influenced by society's emphasis on tolerance. They see that in this country there are now many different religious traditions. They point out, rightly, that we must learn to live together and to respect one another's cultures. To them the exclusive claims of Christianity are not so much a personal affront, but they cannot see how such claims can have any place in today's world.

When someone raises this question, I would have two expectations. First, I would hope to persuade people that the exclusive claims of Christianity are an integral part of our faith. I would want them to see that these claims are not made out of arrogance, but from simple logic; for if Jesus is who he claimed to be, then he is the only way to God. Second, I would want to persuade them not to concentrate on what happens to others who believe this or that or the other, but on what will happen to them and on what they believe for themselves.

Though this is a question that many Christians dread being asked, I can think of few better opportunities for talking about Jesus than answering this question. For he is our answer. Christianity is an exclusive faith because Jesus is unique. However I might well seek to deal on a more general level to start with in order to balance and soften the impact of the exclusivity of what we believe. There is no point in being deliberately provocative or in putting people's backs up unnecessarily. The gospel has an offence of its own, of which its exclusivity is a major part; but we should not add to that offence. Remember our speech is to be 'gracious and seasoned with salt'.

The Fairness of God

The question of those who have never heard is often a red herring, but anything that enables us to speak about the character of God can't be all bad! The fundamental answer to the question is, of course, that God is responsible for judgement. We are not. He has revealed the means by which we can be put right with him and he has told us what he demands of us, namely, repentance and faith. Given this overall character of God it is incomprehensible that he would do anything that was unfair or unjust. The Bible has no clear teaching concerning those who haven't heard of Jesus, but there are hints that God has a way of judging which makes allowances for the light that we have received. The question often assumes that we have a greater understanding of fairness and justice than God does. We forget that our understanding is merely a pale shadow of God's perfect justice, from which our feelings derive. We can therefore confidently leave the matter in his hands. The question I would want to leave with anyone who asks along these lines is: 'You have heard. What do you make of Jesus Christ?'

The Essential Difference

Behind the question concerning the different religions there often lies the hidden question, 'Why should I look at Christianity? Why don't I start with Buddhism or one of the others?' I would aim therefore to demonstrate that Christianity is essentially different from all the other world religions. Religion could be defined as 'the means of getting in touch with God'. Every religion seeks to get us from where we are either to a relationship with God or to some state of perfection or total happiness. All recognise that there is a gulf between us and God. The essential difference is that, whereas all other religions teach that our achieving of this position depends on us, Christianity says that we could never make it on our own, that it depends not on us and what we do, but on God and what he has done. If we were to illustrate it diagrammatically it might look something like Figure 2.

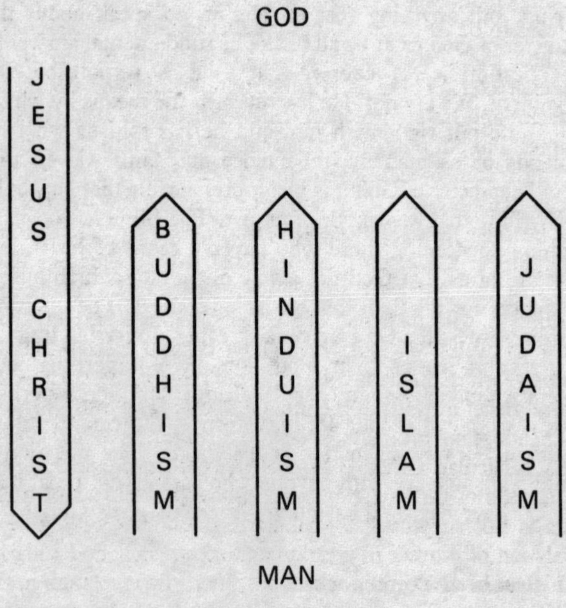

GOD

MAN

[**Figure 2**]

As soon as we begin to understand this difference, it is obvious that Jesus is the key. It is true that some make Christianity into a religion that starts with man, a creed of good works, but New Testament Christianity clearly teaches that our standing before God depends on him and not on us. It is to that uniqueness of Jesus that we must now turn.

The Uniqueness of Jesus' Person

Amongst leaders or founders of world religions Jesus stands apart. Others have claimed similar things but none have been believable. Only Jesus has claimed what he claimed and founded one of the major world religions. The Buddha, Mohammed, Confucius and Moses would not have accepted the worship of others. They saw their task as pointing to another person or another way. When Thomas said to Jesus 'My Lord and my God', Jesus accepted his worship as his due. The claims of Jesus to be God are without parallel in the other religions.

Those claims are substantiated, as we saw in Chapter 10, by his character. There is, furthermore, the evidence of his miracles and his resurrection that we shall look at in the next chapter. For our purposes in this chapter his unique person sets him apart from other leaders. Not only can he tell us about God; he can show us what God is like. If we want to know what God is like, he is like Jesus. His unique person is central to Christianity. Therefore as Judaism and Islam, in particular, deny the claims of Jesus; and as Hinduism, with its multiplicity of gods, and Buddhism, with its denial of a personal God, effectively deny them as well, we must conclude that they are mutually exclusive. If Christianity is true, all religions that deny its central belief in Jesus as the unique Son of God must be false.

That does not mean that every other religion is totally false in every particular. Often Christians give that impression. There are aspects of each religion which show an element of truth. This is not surprising for all have access to God's general revelation of himself in creation and conscience; and Judaism and Islam both accept in whole or in part the revelation in the Old Testament. However the denial of Jesus' unique person is a fundamental flaw and results in each being, if not false in every detail, then false in their central affirmation and in the direction in which they lead people; for they lead people away from Jesus.

The Uniqueness of Jesus' Work

However, there is another equally important aspect of the uniqueness of Jesus. It concerns what he achieved on the cross and it is central to the difference between Christianity and other religions. As we have seen there is a common recognition that there is a gulf between God and us, caused by our sin or rebellion against God. The New Testament claim is that only Jesus has achieved the bridging of that gap. He did it in two ways. He did it first of all in his person, being both fully God and fully man; but he did it also by his death when he took the penalty of our sin on himself and thus removed the barrier between us and God.

Probably the best known illustration of this is the Bridge diagram. If we adapt that to show the difference between Jesus and the world religions we might see it something like this. Diagram 1 shows the gulf betwen us and God and our sin as its cause.

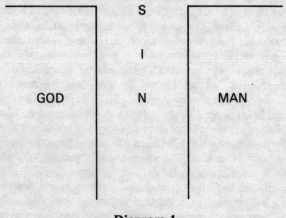

Diagram 1

Diagram 2 shows failed attempts to bridge the gap.

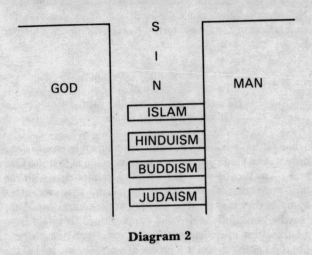

Diagram 2

Diagram 3 shows how Jesus on the cross bridged the gulf between God and Man.

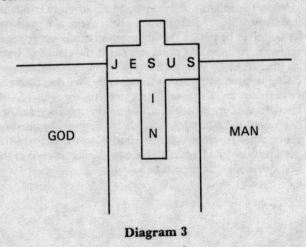

Diagram 3

Jesus, then, stands unique in his work. He is the only one who can deal with the problem that separates us from God. No other religion can cope with sin. Only Jesus as the sinless Son of God was worthy to take the penalty for our sin:

> There was no other good enough
> To pay the price of sin.
> He only could unlock the gate
> Of heaven and let us in.

Now if Jesus is unique in this respect then he must be the only way to God. If the purpose of religion is to unite God and Man, then if the other religions cannot deal with the one thing that divides God and Man, whatever other qualities they may possess, they fail at the central test. A car may be beautifully styled and proportioned. It might have all the latest in-car entertainment and associated gadgets; but if it doesn't move, it is no use as a car. We are told of the great civilisations that have been founded by other faiths and about other great deeds; but if a religion cannot deal with sin it is of no ultimate use.

Many Christians fear being asked about other religions, mainly because we feel ignorant about them. We must not let ourselves be put on the defensive on this issue. It needs sensitive handling and phrasing; but if the claims of Jesus are true, then by definition any religion that denies those claims is incompatible with Christianity. We don't have to be experts on the world religions to see that. Some knowledge of them is useful and worth acquiring but we don't need to know a lot about them. Rather, any question about other religions takes us straight to the heart of the good news of who Jesus is and of what he did. It's one of the best questions that we can be asked.

13: Miracles are Impossible

This is more of an objection than a question. Our modern society which has explanations for so many phenomena has largely ruled out the possibility of the miraculous. At least it has at the one level. At another level we live in a highly superstitious society; people refuse to walk under ladders; if you break a mirror it's a major disaster, even though it is only a piece of silvered glass; millions pore over their horoscopes every day to find out what the future holds; there is a fascination with the paranormal. We live in a schizophrenic society, whose mind says that miracles are not possible, but whose heart tells a different story.

However the objection remains. In part it stems from unfamiliarity – 'I haven't seen a miracle, therefore they are not possible.' In another sense it is based on a high view of science – 'Science has all the answers, and science has no room for the miraculous.' We will look in the next chapter at the supposed conflict between science and Christianity because it has broader implications. Here we will restrict ourselves in particular to the miraculous.

The result of such thinking is of course to make the New Testament a little difficult to swallow. Someone who turns water into wine (popular though the idea is!), who feeds 5,000 people with a few loaves and a couple of fish, who heals the sick and raises the dead, is not easy for us to identify with. We haven't met many people like that! People may like the character of Jesus; they may admire many of the things that he says; but the miracles are a major

125

stumbling-block. They cannot conceive of the stories being true. Therefore the whole of Christianity is thrown into question.

For this very reason many Christians seek to present a miracle-free Jesus. They claim to be demythologising Christianity (that is, taking out the fairy story element). I remember one of my headmasters at school using the school assemblies very soon after he arrived to explain away the Virgin Birth, the existence of angels, the miracles of Jesus and the Resurrection. He was trying to make it easier for cynical teenagers to believe. His motives were entirely genuine, though very misguided, not only because what he was saying was not true, but also because it didn't work! My friends who were not Christians thought he was ridiculous. They saw that the miracles of Jesus are so much an integral part of the New Testament account, that if you remove them there is little left. In their view it was better to be an out and out materialist, rejecting Jesus, God and the miraculous; or, if you were going to believe in God, to believe in a God who could do things we couldn't.

But how far should be we expect to move people who have this objection to Jesus? There are a number of stages in the process, as we have already thought, of moving from unbelief to faith. This is perhaps especially true of those who reject the miraculous. A first stage to aim for might be that they accept that it is as intellectually sound to accept the miraculous as it is to reject it; that their position is as much a position of faith as ours (more of that in a moment). A second stage might be to get them to see that the miracles of Jesus are not just stunts, that they have a much richer character and purpose. A third stage could be to get them to look at the greatest miracle of all, the Resurrection, and examine the evidence for its veracity. Ultimately we want them not only to accept the possibility of the miraculous but to experience the miracle of the new birth in their own lives.

126

The Universe – Open or Closed?

I am writing these chapters during an extended Christmas break which seems to have been marked by a number of detective stories on television. We have had Agatha Christie's Hercule Poirot, Conan Doyle's Sherlock Holmes and many others. One common theme in those I have watched has been murder behind a door which had been locked from the inside, occasionally with the chain attached or the key still in the lock! At the theoretical level the argument over the possibility of the miraculous depends on whether we view our universe as having been locked from the inside or as one that is open to outside forces and involvement.

If our universe is closed and immune to all outside interference then the miraculous is not possible. There may be phenomena which we find difficult to explain; but if the universe is closed, they must be explicable in terms of other factors that exist within the same universe. If however our universe is open, then the miraculous is possible, and becomes defined as anything that happens within our universe that cannot be explained by factors from within. But how do we decide if the universe is open or closed?

Such a decision is a question of faith. Evidence can be put forward for both points of view. We have to judge that evidence and decide for ourselves. Those who reject the miraculous believe that the evidence for the universe being closed is overwhelming, so much so that it is ridiculous to believe in the miraculous. They look at the regular pattern and order of the universe. They see how many supposed miracles do have a scientific explanation. From their point of view they have stepped into the brave new world in which they recognise that we can no longer appeal to any outside force or being, where instead we have to make the best job we can of the world we live in, because there is no one else who can alter it for us. The case, however, is by no means proven. Why is it that for centuries men and women of all races and backgrounds have had a sense within themselves that there is another dimension beyond what we can see and touch and feel? What evidence is there to support their claim that there is no outside involvement in our universe? Though some supposed miracles are capable of explanation, does a scientific explanation also account for the timing and significance of the event? Or, most difficult of all for the rejector of the miraculous, how are we meant to explain the Resurrection of Jesus from the dead? All the evidence points to the reality of that resurrection. The only reason for rejecting it is because of a belief that miracles don't happen. Such a rejection though is not an intellectual one but a fundamentally irrational one.

The case for believing in an open universe is very strong. The burden of proof must lie with those who want to say that it is closed. It is far from irrational at least to allow for the possibility that the universe might be open to outside involvement. Once you have got someone to that point then they must allow for the possibility of the miraculous. We are then in a position to look at some specific examples without being ruled out of court straight away!

The Nature of Jesus' Miracles

Part of the objection to miracles is that people don't like show-offs. The idea of God coming down and doing a few party tricks in front of a fairly primitive and gullible audience is somehow repellent to them – and to most of us as well, I imagine. That is not what Jesus did. The miracles of Jesus are not stunts. A programme I was watching recently was showing how television and film stunts are performed: car crashes, people falling out of helicopters, a man being set on fire and a range of other highly dangerous manoeuvres. When we see them on the screen they take our breath away. When you see how they are done, they still make you breathe deeply and in some ways the admiration grows. However, we all know that they are stunts; that they are meant to impress, but that they are not what they seem. It all depends on timing, on trick photography, on the right

128

camera angle. The miracles of Jesus were not impressive stunts. Each has a purpose.

The purpose of the different miracles varies; sometimes they have a dual purpose. The first three Gospels see Jesus' miracles as being mostly involved with relieving need and with establishing Jesus' identity as having power over evil, disease and nature. He doesn't show them to all and sundry but to those who are open to this message. They confirm his identity and his message. He is, to use the title of Gordon Bridger's book, *The Man from Outside*. As such he needs to demonstrate that his authority comes from above. In John's Gospel the role of the miracles is more closely defined. They are not referred to as miracles but as 'signs' or 'works'. They are 'works' because to the Son of God turning water into wine or raising Lazarus from the dead is all in a day's work. They are miracles to us; but to God they are simply alterations in the normal pattern which he has fixed and which is under his constant control. They are 'signs' because they point to the truth about Jesus. He who can feed 5,000 people with a few fish and loaves is surely 'the Bread of Life'. The one who can open the eyes of a man born blind can justifiably claim to be 'the Light of the World'.

The character of the New Testament miracles becomes clearer still when compared with some of the inventions of later writings. The four Gospels we have in the New Testament were not the only accounts written of the life of Jesus. They are, however, the only ones know to be genuine by the early Church. The others are known as the apocryphal gospels. One of the fascinations of these writers, who were probably writing about 100 years after the death of Jesus, was the gap in Jesus's life between the ages of twelve and thirty, between his appearance at the temple with his parents and the beginning of his public ministry. One of the stories of this period that they recount concerns Jesus playing with clay and making some model birds. He then tells the clay birds to fly away, which they duly do. A miracle, but a miracle without any purpose. That is a stunt.

In his temptations Jesus resisted the temptation to perform a stunt by jumping from the pinnacle of the temple, trusting to the angels to catch him. The character of the miracles of the real Jesus was very different.

The Resurrection of Jesus

Without doubt the main evidence for the miraculous is the resurrection of Jesus. If it didn't happen our faith is without foundation and the question of the miraculous is of merely academic interest. If it did happen then Jesus' claims are vindicated, his work on the cross is authenticated and the miraculous becomes not a possibility but a fact. The point I want to stress is tht this is where we want the focus of any disussion of the miraculous to rest. We are right back in the heart of the good news. New life is possible through the resurrection of Jesus from the dead. We are talking about a central gospel event and the central gospel character. But what is the evidence? What follows is really only a brief summary. You may like to explore it more in a group or by reading on your own (there are many excellent books which give a full treatment to the subject). The evidence centres around three main facts.

FACT 1 – *The Empty Tomb or the Missing Body*

Nobody ever produced the body of the dead Jesus. It would have been to the advantage of many to do so, the Jews and the Romans in particular. What other explanations are there for this apart from the fact that he rose from the dead?

Somebody stole the body – but who?
The Jews – why didn't they produce it?
The Romans – same question, and what motive did they have?
The disciples – would they really have died for what they knew to be a lie?
Grave robbers – why, then, did they steal the worthless body and leave behind the valuable spices?

They went to the wrong tomb – Everybody?
Jesus was laid in the tomb of a well-known member of the Sanhedrin. The Romans, at the request of the Jewish leaders, put a guard around it. Did they all get the wrong tomb? Who put the folded grave clothes there?

FACT 2 – *The Appearances to the Disciples*

Jesus is recorded as appearing to many different groups at different times, in different places and to up to 500 people at a time! (See 1 Corinthians 15, the earliest record we possess of the Resurrection appearances.) What possible explanations are there other than that the risen Jesus was seen by these people?

They were hallucinating – all of them? And so many times? Experts on hallucination reckon that the mindset of the disciples and the physical conditions under which these events took place preclude hallucination as a possible explanation.

Jesus never died – he swooned and recuperated in the cool of the grave. It takes a great deal of faith to believe that a man who had been flogged and crucified, who had been without food for two days, could struggle out of the grave-clothes he was wrapped in, roll back a huge gravestone, evade a Roman guard, walk back to Jerusalem and then convince the disciples not that he had had a lucky escape and needed six months' convalescence, but that he had conquered death and risen to new life! Add to that the eyewitness evidence of the spear piercing his side and the blood and water which flowed from it and the theory dies, just as Jesus most certainly did. The separation of the blood in the way described only takes place in someone well and truly dead. There is no way that that scientific fact could have been known by the author; it is a simple piece of eyewitness testimony.

The disciples invented the stories.
For the same reason that they could not have stolen the

body, they could not have made up the accounts that we have. Not only did they die for what they believed but we have already looked at their emphasis on truth, when thinking about the reliability of the New Testament.

FACT 3 *The Early Church*

The existence of the Church itself is firm evidence that something must have happened to the disciples after the death of Jesus. The Gospels portray the disciples after the crucifixion as a demoralised, frightened group, hiding behind closed and locked doors; afraid, presumably, that what had happened to their leader would happen to them; demoralised to the point of despair by the death of the man for whom they had given up everything. It is a very believable picture. Any other reaction would have been most extraordinary. Yet just a few weeks later they are fearlessly proclaiming that Jesus rose from the dead. They are put in prison. They are persecuted across the length and breadth of the Roman Empire, but they refuse to deny their message that 'Jesus is risen!'

There is no other explanation that fits these facts as well as the explanation that Jesus rose from the dead. It was a miracle. If we rule out the possibility of the miraculous then we have to reach some other conclusion, not because the evidence points in that direction but because our basic assumption means that we cannot reach the most obvious conclusion. Many of those who dismiss the possibility of the miraculous try to adopt the intellectual high ground. They suggest that it is to a primitive mind that the miraculous appeals. They must not be allowed to get away with that deception. It is arguable that to allow for the possibility of the miraculous is much more sound intellectually than to dismiss it.

We must be careful, however, not to overstate our case; it doesn't need it! In particular, with regard to the Resurrection we need to see what the New Testament teaches. There is an element of mystery about it. Jesus appears through locked doors. He is not recognised for some time by the two disciples on the road to Emmaus. He disappears as mysteriously as he appears. The New Testament presents a risen Jesus, whose original body is nowhere to be found, but who now enjoys a new body, at the same time recognisably the same and yet significantly different. The marks are there in his hands and side. He can eat and talk and be touched. Yet he comes and goes at will regardless of physical obstacles.

The subject of the miraculous is one where it is well worth our while working at understanding the evidence. It is a common objection but once again it can lead us into the heart of the good news as we talk about the resurrection of Jesus. At times people will come up with other theories which we can't immediately fault. That is much more likely to be caused by a gap in our knowledge than by a flaw in the evidence for the resurrection. Remember that our ignorance is an opportunity, not a problem – an opportunity to learn more ourselves and to have another conversation with our friend. Many brains far more agile than yours or mine have wrestled with the evidence over many years and concluded that it is one of the most solid cases for establishing an historical fact that you could hope for. Jesus is alive!

14: Do Science and Christianity Conflict?

The subject of the miraculous takes us naturally into the broader area of science in general and its relationship to Christianity in particular. The objection to the miraculous is often set in the broader feeling that science has now taken the place of religion. We no longer need God, for Science can answer all the questions that we used not to understand; and those it struggles with at the moment it will be able to answer soon. Furthermore Christianity, and the Bible especially, are contradictory to modern science. Creation and evolution, it is suggested, are opposite theories that cannot be reconciled. Science has become the modern idol. As a society we bow down to science and its findings. The television has become its shrine; and countless thousands pay homage week by week. On television at the moment there is an advertisement for a lavatory cleaner. It is scientifically compared with others to see how long it kills germs. The punchline after the product wins first prize is: 'And that's a scientists's verdict.' They are the modern gurus of a section of our society.

To be sure modern science has made huge strides forward which have been of enormous benefit to our society, and which we would be idiotic to deny. However the worship of science, which is basically a worship of our own intellect, is not only an affront to God, it is also an intellectual stance which is hard to maintain. Expectations in this area should centre on exposing the limitations of science, so that people no longer worship it, and on disposing of this artificial conflict that is supposed to exist between it and Christianity. Christians should in no way be anti-science for all truth is God's truth and therefore any discovery of truth is valuable.

The Limitations of Science

The omnipotence and omniscience of science are rarely believed in by true scientists. It is for this reason that many eminent scientists are convinced and devout Christians. Certainly in my student days we would always reckon that it was easier to convince an open-minded scientist of the truth of the gospel than a cynical arts student whose mind was filled with the writings of the existentialists. The membership of the Christian Union certainly reflected that. The true scientist closes no doors and is well aware of the limitations of his method of discovering knowledge. It is the TV or armchair scientist who is the villain of the piece. Our broadcasters have a lot to answer for in this area. The photography on television science programmes is often quite spectacular; the problem comes with the commentary. In a soft, gentle voice the commentator mingles statements of fact, of established theory and of pure speculation without differentiating properly between them. It is a subtle form of brainwashing. The viewer is the victim. Thus there is a generation of viewers whose beliefs about the world they live in have been excessively influenced by a small group of broadcasters.

This may sound a little harsh but we need to face the problem that confronts us. I would far sooner engage in dialogue with an agnostic Professor of science, whose mind is open, than with a TV worshipper who has developed a blind faith in science, for such it is for many. The Professor would be aware of both the strengths and weaknesses of the scientific method. Let's take an example to see what we're talking about.

Imagine for a moment that we are conducting a chemical reaction. To discover what is happening and how it happens the scientist observes the process. Observation is the key to the scientific method. From his observations the scientist produces a theory. He then tests his theory by further experiments, seeking to predict what should happen, according to his theory. If the experiments and the scrutiny of his fellow scientists confirm his theory, it becomes established; and we might then refer to it as a fact. The law of gravity, that we were thinking about in an earlier chapter, would be such a fact.

There are two key words in the description above – 'what' and 'how'. Those two words sum up the range of science. It can describe what things consist of, or what happens when different substances are mixed together. It can also tell us how things came to be the way they are: how a reaction takes place, or how plants grow, for example. There are two similar words which are beyond its range, though – 'why' and 'who'. (I'm using 'why' here in the sense of 'with what purpose' not in the sense 'by what mechanism', which is really the equivalent of 'how'.) You may think I'm arguing over words but the distinction is very important. Let me illustrate.

A scientist could observe the manufacture of plastic plant pots. Assume for a moment that he has never seen such an article before and has no access to outside information. By observation and application of his scientific training he could analyse the substances at the beginning of the process – he could tell us 'what' they consist of. He could also describe 'what' happens when the substances react together and 'how' that reaction takes place. At the end of the process he could give us a further analysis of the composition of the final product, 'what' it was made of. He could not tell us, however, by application of the scientific method, if the final article had any purpose – he could not tell us 'why' it was being made. If it was a modern automated plant and he had not observed any other human being in the factory he could not tell us 'who' was responsible for the process either.

Such an example has obvious limitations because we all know what a plastic plant pot is. However, apply that thinking to the universe in which we live, and what happens? The worshipper of science lives in a closed universe; the factory is locked and bolted and he can only learn about what is going on by observing what happens within it. He has no access to outside knowledge. Certainly he can describe 'what' is happening within that space, in terms of what he can observe. He can also tell us 'how' things happen in the universe. But he cannot tell us 'why', that is if they are purposeful or pointless. He cannot tell us 'who', if anybody, is pulling the strings. This distinction should become clearer as we look at the major area of supposed conflict.

Creation and Evolution

The account of the origin of the world we live in is usually taken to be the central area of conflict between science and Christianity. If we apply the thinking we have just been using, however, the conflict dies away like a storm in a teacup. Science can only tell us what our world consists of and how it came to be the way it is now. It is beyond its powers to tell us whether or not our lives have any purpose or whether or not there is a master planner behind the universe.

If it is important to understand the limitations of science, it is equally important to understand the nature of the Bible, if we are to avoid an unnecessary conflict between the two. The problems are not only on the scientist's side. Christians who treat the Bible as a scientific textbook are equally to blame for the conflict that is seen by many. In looking at the book of Genesis in particular we need to remember both to whom it was written and for what purpose. This is not to doubt that it is the revealed Word of God. It is merely to ask 'To whom was God speaking at the time?' Presumably it is fair to assume that he would not speak to them in a language that they could not understand.

The book of Genesis was written for a primitive people, to whom the ideas of modern science would have been incomprehensible. It was written for a special purpose. If we examine the first two chapters that tell the story of the Creation, the preoccupation is clear. The writer, and therefore God as author, is concerned first with the question 'Who?' and second with the question 'Why?' If you read Genesis 1 and count the number of times the word 'God' occurs it is quite staggering. 'In the beginning God . . .' and so it continues. He is the subject. Who was responsible for the world in which they lived? God was. It was his Creation. If we look on then to the climax of the story, we find that it concerns the creation of mankind and especially our purpose. The means of creation is not dwelt on. The purpose is the major factor. In Chapter 1 it is that we might fill the earth and subdue it. In Chapter 2 the emphasis is on relationships, with the making of woman. Whose world is it? It is God's world because he made it. What is our role in the world? It is, under the authority of God, to rule over the world and to live in relationship with him and with one another. In a nutshell that is the message of Genesis 1 and 2.

The chapters record the Creation but are not primarily concerned with the mechanism of it; though even there the conflict is more imaginary than real. Genesis 1, in particular, is remarkable for its closeness to the order in which scientists believe that life developed. It begins in the waters: 'And God said "Let the waters bring forth swarms of living creatures, and let birds fly across the firmament of the heavens" ' (Genesis 1.20). The phrase 'bring forth' is an interesting one to anyone who wants to suggest that the Bible does not conceive of Creation being in any way a process.

We need to be careful, too, in our interpretation of the time element in Genesis 1; for though God could most certainly have created the universe in seven days, we need only believe that if it is what Genesis 1 is clearly teaching. If it was a modern scientific textbook then we would have to interpret it in that way. In scientific terms 'an evening and a morning' equal a day, twenty-four hours. However we are not dealing with a scientific textbook; we are dealing with a piece of ancient literature, inspired by God to be relevant both to the people who first received it and to us today. The Bible's attitude to time is not always the same as ours. 'With the Lord one day is as a thousand years, and a thousand years as one day' (2 Peter 3.8). Christians who accept the Bible's authority differ on this issue; but I cannot see that Genesis 1 demands that we believe in Creation in seven periods of twenty-four hours.

Given the above, there need be no conflict between the accounts of science and the Bible. The two are telling the same story but from wholly different perspectives and answering totally separate questions. I have always found the late Professor Mackay's illustration of the television very helpful here. If I am watching *Match of the Day* on television, there are at least two ways of describing what is happening. There is a technical description which describes how the television picture is translated into a form which can be transmitted, which can then be decoded by my television set so that it sends little particles through the tube in the set, forming a coloured picture on the screen identical to that which the camera recorded. However there is another explanation, which to those who like football is much more interesting. It is that John Motson is at Anfield describing the game between Liverpool and Spurs and that I am watching it at home, hoping that Spurs, against all the odds, can pull off a famous victory! The two descriptions are almost totally different but both are equally valid. They are answering different questions. Professor MacKay argued persuasively that science and the Bible give very different but complementary accounts of the origin of our world. *That* God made the world is central to the Bible's teaching. *How* he did it, though, is of no real importance. God's revelation always has practical outworkings in our lives. Whether God made the world in seven days or millions of years makes absolutely no difference to any moral decision that I have to make today.

Seeing the complementary nature of the relationship has two important effects. First, it frees us from any idea of a 'God of the gaps' theology. According to this way of thinking God is the explanation for anything that we cannot explain. With the growth of scientific knowledge room for such a God was becoming very restricted – the gaps were fast disappearing. The Bible has no such view of God, however. Many non-Christians assume that this is what we believe and sometimes our attitude to science gives them reason to believe that. Second, it should give us a thirst for knowledge about the world that God has made. The command to fill the world and subdue it has not been rescinded. I think of a Christian friend from university days. He was a research chemist, in the area of mass spectroscopy (if I have the right technical name!). His work involved him in exploring to the frontiers of human knowledge and beyond, making and trying to predict the behaviour of new molecules. After a hard day in the labs he would often drop in for a cup of coffee late at night. I can remember well a few occasions when he came into my room beaming all over his face and saying 'Kim, I've subdued another molecule today!' Combining that positive attitude and his role as a Methodist lay preacher with a firm commitment to teaching people the Bible, he is to me the symbol of how there is no real conflict between science and Christianity if we understand them both correctly.

15: Suffering and a God of Love?

The problem of suffering is one of the greatest obstacles that we will have to face in persuading people to believe. Not only is it a complex issue which arises in many different forms, it is also a question that often troubles us as Christians. If we have been looking at pointers rather than answers so far in these last chapters, then we need to be even more aware here that what follows is an outline, a basic framework for our thinking, and in no sense an 'answer' to the problem. For in fact there is no answer; and that needs to be one of the first things that we admit when coping with this subject. Our honesty in acknowledging that we still struggle with the issue will be respected by any genuine enquirer.

The reality of suffering is difficult for us to escape these days. Our television screens and newspapers are filled with pictures of starving children, or disasters at home and abroad, of grieving relatives at the funerals of those killed by terrorists and of other actrocities. Few of us will not have experienced some form of suffering, by way of disease or bereavement, in our own lives or in the lives of those who are close to us. The thought arises in every mind, 'It shouldn't be like this.' In the mind of the non-Christian that soon becomes, 'There can't be a God of love if the world is so full of suffering.'

The question arises in many different forms and is asked from various perspectives. Some, sadly, seem to have little feeling and yet raise this issue as a smokescreen, knowing

that Christians often find it difficult to answer. Much more
frequently it is a heartfelt reservation, stemming not so
much from personal experience as from a sense of iden-
tification with others. Sometimes it comes up as the result
of a personal experience that has had a profound impact on
the life of the questioner, as with couples whose children
die at an early age. However it arises it must be dealt with
sensitively, particularly with any who are still coping with
some catastrophe in their own experience. It is a subject
where the principle of listening and learning is especially
important.

The form of the question varies along different lines. For
some their objection is to God – 'If he's all-powerful, why
doesn't he stop it?' For others it is the cause, be it general or
particular, which troubles them – 'Why suffering?' and
'Why that person?' or 'Why me?' There are many, too, who
think that Christians must pretend that suffering doesn't
exist, that we are burying our heads in the sand.

Our expectations in dealing with this question cannot
possibly be to tie it up neatly, like a parcel, with a piece of
ribbon and a bow. However, even though it is a hard issue
to cope with, we do have some very important things to say.
We won't necessarily say all of them in every case; but we
will want to show that Christianity faces up to the problem
squarely, that the Bible does give us pointers towards the
cause of suffering and God's purpose in allowing it to
continue in his world. Above all we will want to point
people to the sufferings of Jesus, to the fact that he
understands, from the inside.

The Bible's Realism

If Christians are ever guilty of burying their heads in the
sand, the Bible certainly isn't. In one of the great passages
on suffering in the New Testament (Romans 8.18–26) Paul
uses three phrases that express perfectly the world we live
in and our feelings towards it. He speaks of our being
'subjected to futility'. The word implies emptiness, a sense

of purposelessness and frustration, an idea that finds its expression today in unemployment, alcoholism and all forms of escapism. He goes on to talk about the world's 'bondage to decay', a phrase that sums up our inner cities, our proneness to disease, the way nothing remains new for long – from a child's toy to a peace treaty between nations. In a vivid picture he then describes the creation as being like a woman in labour, 'groaning in travail'.

This realism is reflected throughout the Bible. The psalmists complain to God about the things they have to endure. The historians record bitter family wrangles, the grief of bereavement and the suffering of the people in exile. The gospel writers tell of Jesus's scourging, mocking and crucifixion. It also recognises the problem of trying to explain suffering. It gives no simple answers but there are pointers.

The Cause of Suffering

Who's to blame? Is it God's fault? Certainly he allows it; for, if he is the omnipotent Creator, he must be able to bring an end to suffering if he chose to. More than that, Paul tells us indirectly in the same passage that it is God who has subjected the creation to futility, but that he's done it 'in hope', for a purpose. However that doesn't mean that he caused suffering. It cannot be his fault. The fault must be ours. Sin is the cause of suffering; but the link between the two is not necessarily direct. There are two opposite viewpoints on this link which may help to clarify it for us. Some see it as a simple link – I suffer in a particular way because of a particular sin; it is God's punishment. There are those who suggest that this is only a primitive understanding, but the question 'Why me?' which we so often ask shows that it is still very much in our thinking. That question reveals that we see our suffering as God's specific punishment. We want to know why he thinks that we are worse than others and what we have done to merit such displeasure. The alternative viewpoint is that suffering is random and never deserved – there is no link. The New Testament rejects both extremes.

When Jesus is told about the suffering of some Galileans who were slaughtered by Pilate's soldiers while they were in the act of making a sacrifice to God, he asks them: 'Do you think that these Galileans were worse sinners than all the other Galileans, because they suffered thus? I tell you, No.' He goes on to remind them of another incident in which a tower fell on some passers-by. He asks an identical question and gives the same answer, 'I tell you, No.' He rejects clearly the simple link. However in each case he goes on to say 'but unless you repent you will all likewise perish' (Luke 13.1–5), thus affirming that there is a link.

Sometimes the link is direct. If I murder someone I suffer as my freedom is taken away. More often it is indirect – my suffering is caused by the sin of another. The sin of Hitler and his associates caused horrendous suffering for the Jews in the holocaust. Even in famines, which seem like natural disasters, there is often an underlying cause in the selfishness of 'the haves', the stubborness of a government or the way we have altered climates by our destruction of the environment. However, often the link is not direct, nor is it clear, as when children are born handicapped, or when they die suddenly and inexplicably. In all of these indirect causes we speak normally about 'innocent victims'; but is there such a thing? Jesus' warning seems to indicate that all of us deserve in some way to suffer, that the link between that suffering and a particular sin may not exist, but that a link surely does exist between our rebellion against God and our deserving to be punished. Paul's teaching in Romans 8 shows that the whole of creation is off course, that the cause is our sinfulness, but that God's purpose is one of hope.

The Bible's view and ours are very different. We see the magnitude of our suffering and think that there cannot be a God of love. The Bible sees the magnitude and seriousness of our sin, that we deserve to be punished. Yet alongside that it also tells us of a God of love who has a purpose in allowing suffering, that we might turn from what we know to be wrong and trust in him.

Before we move on to look at this purpose in more detail it is important to recognise the right context for developing this line of thinking. Jesus himself used it with a group who came raising a general point. There is no hint of any of them being personally involved in the incident. When he met those who were more closely involved we see less challenge and more compassion. He is our model.

The Purpose of Suffering

To many suffering is the proof that life has no purose. The existentialist position is founded on this view of the world. Life in a closed universe is pointless. We live in a crazy, irrational world. Therefore, they say, we must create meaning for ourselves. The Bible takes the opposite view. Life has purpose. We are made to live in relationship to God. We, however, have rebelled against him and have lost sight of this purpose as a result. Suffering is seen as one of God's signposts to show us that we are heading in the wrong direction and to point us back to himself. Many reject the signpost. Their reaction is one of anger, self-pity or increasing rebellion. Others read the signpost and follow it. A young couple I know who had lost their baby in a 'cot death' found Christ through the trauma.

We must not delude ourselves that what we have thought about here is an answer to the problem. It goes some way to helping us to live with the issue but it does not remove all of the mystery by any means. The purposes and reasoning of God are beyond us. Often our thinking is clouded by 'If I were God, I would . . .' We constantly limit God and think of him within a human framework and value system. There is bound to be mystery. There are bound to be issues we don't fully understand. With this subject as with all the others we have looked at, we need to remember that our goal is not to provide complete answers, but to show that there is a framework of understanding within which our suffering can seem to have some purpose. There is also the biblical framework of time which shows that our present suffering is temporary, that one day there will be a new heaven and a new earth. In this new creation there will be no more crying or pain; for God's purposes in allowing us to suffer have a long-term goal. Our problems with accepting suffering stem not only for our underestimating sin, as we have seen, but also from our false perspective on time, where the immediate is all that is significant. It is interesting that it is in our Western world that we are most aware of suffering as an argument against the existence of God. In other cultures where the attitude to time and possessions is different their view of suffering is very different too.

The Supreme Example of Suffering

On many occasions I might well not refer to any of the issues raised above when talking to a non-Christian about suffering. Even when I do it is with this point that I would want to conclude and on which I would wish to concentrate. It is quite simply to say that Jesus knows what it is like to suffer. He lived in our messy world for over thirty years and finally died the death of a common criminal. He was deserted by his friends. He was brutally beaten and ridiculed. He was hung on a cross in what is commonly recognised to be one of the most barbaric and cruel forms of execution that man has ever devised for his fellow man.

For many the objection against God is undergirded by the strong feeling, 'It's all right for him.' God is in his heaven and all is right with the world; only it isn't. To such people God is seen as callous and uninvolved. Jesus, especially through his death on the cross, shows us not only that God cares, but also that he understands, that he's been through it. He is involved. A friend pointed out to me recently the difference between the image of the Buddha, cross-legged, eyes closed, oblivious to the reality of the world and its suffering, and the New Testament portrait of Jesus spread out on a cross, in agony of body, mind and spirit, immersed in our world, its sinfulness and shame.

Once again this is not an 'answer', but it is highly relevant. If asked, 'How do you live with the tension of believing in a God of love while there is so much suffering in the world?', my answer is that it is Jesus who helps me to cope. If God's way of sorting out the mess that we have made of his world had to involve Jesus in suffering as he did, then suffering must have some part to play. It must be necessary in some way that I don't fully understand. If there was any other way then surely God would have chosen it for his Son.

As we seek to put this and the other points to people our attitude should be sensitive and positive. Sensitivity is obviously required. A positive attitude is also essential. Suffering is perceived as wholly negative in our society because it robs us of everything that we consider to be our right, happiness, security, comfort. It's easy for us to pick up this negative mindset as we approach the subject. It is however another opportunity to talk about Jesus. Admittedly it is the sombre side of his life and ministry that we are drawn to; but in the paradox of much of Scripture, it is this sombre message which contains the seed of life. When dealing with this question, perhaps, above all others, we need to determine to know nothing except Jesus Christ and him crucified.

16: And the Little One Said . . .

In the last few chapters we have looked at some of the major questions that are asked by those objecting to or questioning Christianity. However there are a host of other questions that are asked. Often they seem small and fairly innocuous but they can be the ones that simply will not go away. We will look at three of these 'little' questions in this chapter.

Do I have to Go to Church to Be a Christian?

There are two common thought patterns which lie behind this and associated questions. The first is based on an aversion to the Church. David Watson, the evangelist, quoted the student who displayed a banner which read 'Jesus, Yes. The Church, No!' For some this aversion to the Church is based on bad experiences of the Church. A negative impression created by an unhelpful vicar or by the dowdiness and irrelevance of church services can become a major obstacle. For others the problem has historical roots. They look at the role of the Church at certain stages of history and cannot accept that such a body could possibly be in any way representative of God. They might be thinking of the Spanish Inquisition or some of the early missionary enterprises which stamped out all local culture. For some it is contemporary conflicts, such as that in Northern Ireland, or the seeming disunity and disarray of some of the major denominations, perhaps especially the Church of England to which I belong.

The second line of thinking cannot see the necessity of the

Church. To those of this persuasion faith is a private matter. It has to do with their personal behaviour. It is these things, they say, which make them a Christian, not going to church – 'And anyway, many people who don't go to church are much better people than those who do.'

Our first reaction in both cases must be to plead guilty on behalf of the Church. We cannot deny that many of these objections contain large elements of truth. However in both cases the problems stem from misunderstandings of what it means to be a Christian, of how one becomes a Christian and of the nature of the Church.

Going to church does not make one a Christian, just as dressing up in a Spurs football outfit would not make me a member of the Spurs football team. Doing Christian things, whether it be going to church or trying to keep the ten commandments, does not make anyone a Christian. A Christian is someone who has a relationship with God through Jesus Christ. This is news to many of those who are not yet Christians. It is also a major element of the good news and therefore the question, though always embarrassing because it has so much truth in it, is a good opportunity for leading into productive areas of discussion. Remember that is where we are always trying to head – back to Jesus. Ultimately we are asking people to decide about Jesus, not the Church. We might often have to say, 'Yes, the Church is not much to write home about; but what about Jesus? What is your reaction to him?'

There are two areas concerning the nature of the Church with which we may well have to deal in answering these objections. The first concerns the make-up of the Church. The outsider often feels the Church is a group of people who are saying, 'Look at us, we are better than you.' Nothing could be further from the truth in biblical terms, though sadly we sometimes give this impression. The primary qualification for joining the Church is to recognise our own unworthiness and need of God's forgiveness. The Church is therefore a society of sinners not of saints (in the popular meaning of the word). We should not therefore expect the Church or its members to be perfect. However, Jesus also made it clear that the visible Church would always be a mixed bag, that not everyone who called him 'Lord, Lord' would enter the kingdom of heaven, that the kingdom was like a field planted with wheat and weeds. It is quite clear from the moral stance of some in the Church, and from the beliefs others proclaim, that any link between New Testament Christianity and what they profess is tenuous to say the least. Similarly, in history the Church has been hijacked by many unscrupulous types for a variety of political reasons and for personal advancement. We cannot possibly defend every action of the leaders of the Church, past or present. We must acknowledge the failure openly while at the same time setting it in the context above.

The second misunderstanding relates to how we join the Church. Many understand it to be separate from a commitment to Christ. However in all the New Testament images of what it means to be a Christian, or of the nature of the Church, being a Christian entails automatic membership of the Church, whether we like it or not. If I am born again as a child of God or adopted as his son or daughter, then I become a member of his family. He is my heavenly Father and other Christians are my brothers and sisters. You probably know the saying, 'God gave me my family. Thank God I can choose my friends!' Well he's given us our spiritual family as well. If the Church is a body and every Christian is baptised into the one body, then whether I'm a hand or an arm, a vital organ or the little toe, I am part of the body. If the Church is an army and I sign up as a soldier of Christ then I must serve with my fellow-soldiers. It cannot be a one-man private army.

Going to church does not make a person a Christian. Being a Christian, however, automatically entails being a member of the Church, which will always be an imperfect assortment of sinners, until she is presented without spot or blemish as the Bride of Christ when he returns.

Aren't All Good People Christians?

This question is closely connected to the one we have just considered. Doing good things does not make a person a Christian. It is a matter of a relationship with God through Jesus Christ. However, I choose to deal with it separately because there is an additional element which it gives an opportunity to clarify.

This line of thinking is deeply embedded in the British psyche. You meet it in my job when you take funerals. 'He was a real Christian. He never went to church; but he was always kind to people. He never did anyone any harm.' Now it is natural to idolise a loved one immediately after they have died. However it is symptomatic of a general attitude which makes us resistant to the gospel. We refuse to accept our basic sinfulness and rebellion against God. We judge ourselves not by God's absolute standards but by comparing ourselves with other people. In one sense the answer to the question is, 'Yes, all good people are Christians; but there are no completely good people.' There is after all no such thing as someone who never did anyone any harm. Compared with others there may be many who seem good to us; but by God's standards they are not. None of us are. 'All have turned aside, together they have gone wrong; no one does good, not even one' (Romans 3.12). A test of the first three of the ten commandments or of the first great commandment that we love God with all our heart, mind, soul and strength, is a test that none of us could pass.

God's requirement of us in the gospel is that we repent, acknowledging our rebellion and turning from what we know to be wrong, and believe, trusting in Jesus and his cross for our forgiveness and new life. If I think of myself as 'a good person', I will never be able to respond to the good news. Once again the question has led us back to the heart of the good news.

Isn't Faith Just Psychological?

'It's all in your mind'. 'It makes a difference for you because you are convinced it is true'. It's amazing how powerful the human mind is when it is truly convinced of something. So goes the reasoning, and there is power in it. Indians lie on beds of nails and walk over burning coals. Patients who think they are going to get better have a much better chance of recovery. It is not unreasonable to suggest that faith might be a similar trick of the mind, useful because it has a beneficial effect on us, but not ultimately real.

There is no arguing against this objection on its own grounds. It may or may not be true. If however on other grounds, as we have been seeking to establish in these last chapters, Christianity is demonstrably true, then even though it could be a psychological trick, it isn't; because it is faith in the truth. The objection does, however, give us an opportunity to talk about the nature of faith which is an area of much misunderstanding.

Your may well have had one of these two statements made to you. 'I wish I had your faith. I'd really love to believe, but I can't'; or 'It's happened for you. You've experienced it and I haven't. I suppose I'll just have to wait until it happens to me.' Both reveal a fundamental misunderstanding of the nature of faith. They treat it as a substance. You've either got it or you haven't. It is of course nothing of the sort. Faith is an ability that we all have. It is a matter of the will, of choice. We all have faith, the question is where we put it. Many see life as a game of roulette. They are spreading their risk and putting their chips on as many squares as possible. We are asking them to put every chip they possess onto one square. It's not that they can't. It is either that they don't see why they should, or that they don't want to.

From another angle faith is like a muscle. We all have them, but they grow stronger with exercise. All of us have a basic belief whether we are fully conscious of it or not, whether it be a fixed belief or one that changes day by day. It may be a belief in ourselves, that somehow we'll muddle through. It might be a faith in human reason or in the goodness of mankind; but all of us have faith.

There is, therefore, no such problem as 'I can't believe'.

The problem is that I choose to believe in something other than Jesus. I will not give up my other beliefs to which I've grown accustomed in order to place my whole trust in Christ. It's not that it hasn't happened to me, it is that I have been resisting it. But I also won't own up to that. I camouflage it. I hide behind a smokescreen of questions and objections. I try to make you feel guilty because you have a faith which I would like to have. We must not be fooled by that deception.

And Finally . . .

Probably the most difficult thing about dealing with people's questions is knowing if they are genuine or merely a smoke-screen behind which they can hide to avoid the challenge of the gospel. If in doubt it is always best to treat the question as genuine, making sure wherever possible that you bring the subject back to Jesus. It is often their reaction to him which will show if they are genuine or not. If they are prepared to talk about him, to read about him and to grapple with our one question 'Who do you think Jesus is?', then we must grapple with their questions as best we can. If they refuse to look seriously at the person of Jesus then, after a while, we should perhaps wonder if our time could be better spent. There are many who are hungry to hear the gospel; it may well be right to move on to them. Certainly Paul always went to the Jews first, his most natural port of call; but if, after a while, they refused to listen or examine the claims of Jesus seriously then he moved on to those who did.

Alongside the work of prayer and our need to be living examples, both individually and corporately, of Jesus Christ, there are few more vital tasks for the Church today than to provide answers to people's questions and to present them with a reasonable faith. However, one task which *is* more vital is to bring them to a living relationship with Jesus Christ. Answering their questions will almost certainly be part of that process as our lives touch. However, getting their lives to touch the life of Christ must be our ultimate aim. Hence the question, 'Who do you think Jesus is?'; and when they answer it affirmatively, 'Then what are you going to do about him?'

It is not within the scope of this book to give a detailed description of how to lead someone to Christ. We have however in recent chapters discussed most of the central elements of the good news. If we have covered this ground and our work is based in prayer, then the time will come when people want to respond. I close therefore with one simple tip about how to lead someone to Christ. It is unlikely that all their questions will have been answered. Mine haven't been yet so I doubt theirs will be! However if they have got to a point where it seems much more reasonable to believe than not to believe; where they are prepared to admit their rebellion against God, to turn from what they know to be wrong, to trust in Jesus' death on the cross, and to submit their lives to Jesus as Lord, then there is something very simple that we can do with them. We may not feel able to take them through the steps to faith on our own; but we could read with them one of the many booklets that have been produced on how to become a Christian. They will contain all the information we need and can easily be kept in a pocket or wallet or handbag. They are available from most Christian bookshops or church bookstalls.

There is no thrill I know equal to that of leading someone to Christ. It is even more thrilling if the person concerned is someone whose life we have touched over a period of time, so that they have become very dear to us. We don't have to be experts to do it. We don't have to be able to explain all at once the different arguments we have been thinking about in these final chapters. The most important thing is that we are thrilled with the good news ourselves, that we see ourselves as good news people, so that when our lives touch the lives of others, something of the good news is communicated; be it through the way we live, the things we say, or the way we help them to grapple with their questions and objections. That's the natural touch.